WAGING THE BATTLE
AGAINST
DRUNK DRIVING

WAGING THE BATTLE AGAINST DRUNK DRIVING

Issues, Countermeasures, and Effectiveness

Gerald D. Robin

PRAEGER

New York
Westport, Connecticut
London

Library of Congress Cataloging-in-Publication Data

Robin, Gerald D.
    Waging the battle against drunk driving : issues, countermeasures,
and effectiveness / Gerald D. Robin.
        p. cm.
    Includes bibliographical references and index.
    ISBN 0-275-94040-3 (pbk. : alk. paper)
    1. Drunk driving—United States. I. Title.
KF2231.R63   1991
345.73 '0247—dc20
[347.305247]   91-2505

British Library Cataloguing in Publication Data is available.

A hardcover edition of *Waging the Battle against Drunk Driving* is available
from the Greenwood Press imprint of Greenwood Publishing Group, Inc.
(Contributions in Criminology and Penology, 32; ISBN 0-313-27856-3).

Library of Congress Catalog Card Number: 91-2505
ISBN: 0-275-94040-3

First published in 1991

Praeger Publishers, One Madison Avenue, New York, NY   10010
An imprint of Greenwood Publishing Group, Inc.

Printed in the United States of America

∞™

The paper used in this book complies with the
Permanent Paper Standard issued by the National
Information Standards Organization (Z39.48-1984).

P

To my father, Jack Robin, the greatest man I know.
    To my loving and wise mother, Sylvia.
To the best brother in the world, Gary Robin,
    with whom I am forever and inextricably bonded,
And to Leonard Stein, my true mentor,
    whose guiding hand is with me in every word I write.

Contents

Illustrations

PHOTOS

EXHIBITS

Preface

The development of this book was prompted by and reflects a number of related concerns and objectives. Foremost, it grew out of a need to recognize the serious social problem of drunk driving (DWI) for what it unequivocally is: one of the most common types of illegal conduct that for too long has been overlooked as a subject for criminological inquiry. What is most noteworthy about this offense at the present is the nature of our changing attitudes, reactions, and practices in dealing with it. Accordingly, my priority has been to present a succinct, comprehensive, and balanced analysis of society's emerging response to the phenomenon of DWI, the offenders involved, and the factors responsible for challenging and changing the status quo mentality and policies of benign neglect regarding the crime and its perpetrators. I have thus placed into an integrated perspective the various developments, innovations, issues, and controversies that constitute and identify the contemporary anti-drunk driving campaign in the United States. This multifaceted reform agenda is characterized by an eclectic variety of drunk driving countermeasures based on a deterrence model of containment.

The first two chapters are used to define drunk driving (DWI) and related concepts, to comment on its prevalence and fateful conse-quences, and to describe the background of and set the stage for im-plementing new strategies, techniques, and procedures. In the following chapters the step-by-step detection, processing, and disposition of offenders is the framework for examining the substantive parameters of change. The efficacy of the individual countermeasures have been systematically evaluated throughout, as appropriate. The last chapter is an assessment of the success of the diversified reform efforts taken as a whole. While it is premature to make any conclusive observations or final judgments in this regard, it is evident from the events described herein that we have at least and at last turned a decisive corner in our toleration of and response to the crime of drunk driving. It may be prophetic that just as this volume is going to press, the Centers for Disease Control has reported a 12 percent decrease in the number of intoxicated drivers involved in fatal crashes from 1982 through 1989.

Much of the existing literature on drunk driving is fragmented, scattered over several disciplinary areas, contained in rather specialized sources, and intertwined with the broader problem of alcoholism as a separate issue. The research entailed in preparing this book therefore necessitated carefully culling, scrutinizing, and synthesizing an extensive, overlapping, and diffuse body of material for the purpose at hand. I have striven to produce a document that is informative, educational, interesting, and useful to students instructors, researchers, justice system personnel, treatment practitioners, and the victims of drunk driving themselves.

Acknowledgments

I am indebted to the University of New Haven for providing me with a research assistant during the period that this book was being researched and prepared. I thank my research assistant, Gary Schreter, for his outstanding efforts, performance, and contribution to this book. In addition, this research project was supported, in part, by a UNH Summer Faculty Fellowship sponsored by the generosity of Mr. and Mrs. Roland Bixler.

1

The Drunk Driving Problem

DEFINING DRUNK DRIVING

Legally, drunk driving or driving while intoxicated (DWI) is defined by state law as driving with a specific amount or percentage of alcohol in the blood—the individual's Blood Alcohol Level (BAL), which can be measured through breath, urine, or blood tests. By 1989, all but four states had adopted .10 as the BAL at which drivers are considered legally drunk.[1] The rationale for making .10 the criterion for road-drunkenness is that at this BAL the driving skills of virtually everyone are significantly diminished—such individuals are accidents waiting to happen. Over 80 percent of all alcohol-related fatal crashes involve legally intoxicated drivers.[2]

.10 Blood Alcohol Level

A .10 BAC (Blood Alcohol Concentration) means that alcohol constitutes one-tenth of one percent of all blood in the driver's system. While this amount may not seem large, a .10 BAC has an adverse effect on reaction time, vision, judgment, and the ability to brake and control speed; as a depressant, even small quantities of alcohol, in any form,[3] reduces sensorimotor coordination.[4] Moreover, drivers with a .10 BAC are seven times more likely to be involved in an accident than are sober drivers; the risk of an accident is twenty-five times greater at .15 BAL (about eight drinks in an hour) and increases 100-fold at .20 BAC.[5] Not only does the likelihood of a crash occurring increase as the BAL increases, but the higher the BAC the more serious the crash.[6] Commonly observed BAC levels of arrested drunk drivers are in fact much higher than the .10 minimum. The average BAC of 7,000 first-offender drunk drivers in Albuquerque was .168. And in New York, which requires that all persons with a prior drunk driving conviction be screened for alcohol problems, the average BAL of 300 multiple-offenders interviewed in 1985 was .20.[7]

What It Takes to Be Drunk

The BAC level is a result, primarily, of three factors: the amount of food in the stomach (more food slows the rate at which alcohol is absorbed into the bloodstream), the rate at which liquor is consumed over a given time period, and body weight.[8] On an empty stomach, it would take about five (80-proof one-ounce) drinks consumed in an hour for a 150-pound person to be legally intoxicated, that is, to reach a .10 BAC (see Figure 1.1). A 120-pound person could reach .10 by downing four drinks in an hour, while it would take six drinks for a 180-pound person to do so. The same individuals would have to consume considerably more liquor to reach .10 if they had recently eaten, were eating and drinking at the same time, or if the drinking interim were extended.[9] Half of the drunk drivers involved in fatal crashes have a BAC of .20—twice the legal limit for intoxication.[10] To have a .20 BAL, a 160-pound person would have to consume eleven drinks of 80-proof liquor in one hour on an empty stomach.

Lower BAC Levels

As part of the anti-drunk driving movement discussed throughout this book, reformers have urged states to reduce the threshold of driver intoxication from .10 to .08, a more stringent standard commonly used in many European countries, but such efforts have been stifled by the alcohol industry and business community, who claim that doing so would needlessly penalize the social drinker.[11] As of 1989, only Maine, Oregon, and Utah had adopted a .08 BAC, and six other states (including California) were considering doing so.[12] No state has yet implemented the American Medical Association position favoring a .05 standard of intoxication, even though recent studies show that most people become noticeably driving-impaired at

Figure 1.1
Allstate "Amount of Liquor It Takes To Be Drunk"

ESTIMATED AMOUNT OF 80 PROOF LIQUOR NEEDED TO REACH APPROXIMATE GIVEN LEVELS OF ALCOHOL IN THE BLOOD

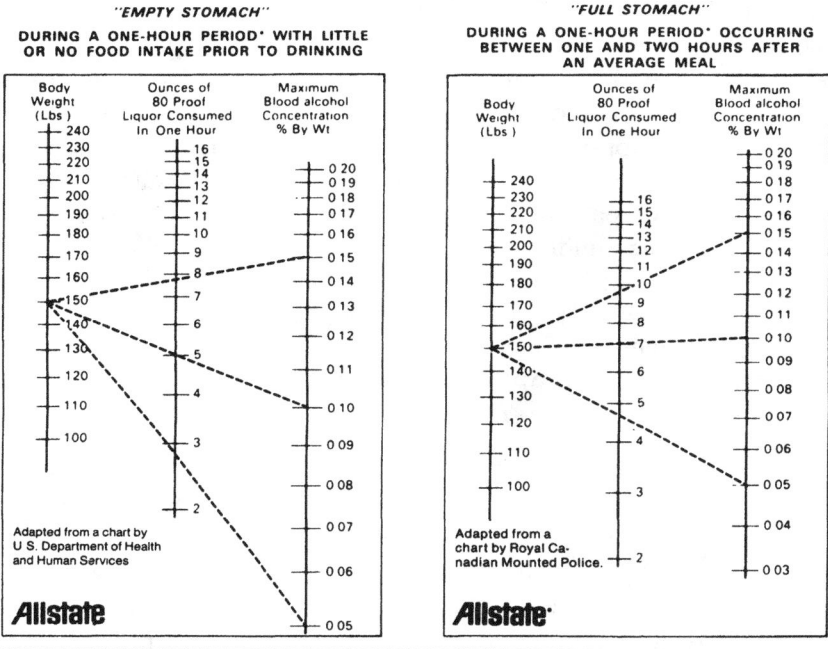

"EMPTY STOMACH"
DURING A ONE-HOUR PERIOD* WITH LITTLE OR NO FOOD INTAKE PRIOR TO DRINKING

"FULL STOMACH"
DURING A ONE-HOUR PERIOD* OCCURRING BETWEEN ONE AND TWO HOURS AFTER AN AVERAGE MEAL

Adapted from a chart by U.S. Department of Health and Human Services

Adapted from a chart by Royal Canadian Mounted Police.

Allstate

Allstate

To determine the approximate average number of standard drinks needed in a one-hour period to reach 0.10 percent, draw a line from BODY WEIGHT to 0.10 percent. The line will intersect the average number of ounces needed to produce 0.10 percent. Follow the same procedure to determine the amount of liquor needed to reach other blood-alcohol concentrations. Figure courtesy of Allstate Insurance Company.

this BAL and that the risk of a .05 driver having an accident is five times that of a nondrinking driver.[13] A .05 drunkenness BAC might very well put a damper on social drinking at commercial establishments; a University of Minnesota study of alcoholic beverages served on the premises found that the typical patron in bars or taverns consumed 2.5 drinks in an average seventy-five minute stay, producing an average BAL of .05.[14]

Driving While Impaired

Recognizing the potential danger posed by drivers with a BAL of less than .10, in several states drivers with a BAC between .05-.09 can be charged with the lesser offense of "driving while *impaired*" (which is not a DWI offense); New York, for example, has a lesser charge, "driving with impaired ability," that only requires a BAC of .05.[15] The federal government has established a .04 drunkenness BAL for truckers and other commercial vehicle operators, which the states must also apply to this special group of drivers by 1993 in order to continue receiving Federal highway funds.[16] Some states, such as Wisconsin, have passed "not-a-drop" laws applicable to minors, whereby anyone under the legal drinking age who has any measurable BAC while operating a motor vehicle—who are not sober (0.00 BAC)—can have their driver's license suspended.[17] The National Academy of Science estimates that if no one drove after drinking, about 11,000 traffic deaths a year could be averted.[18]

ALCOHOL-RELATED FATALITIES

Alcohol is one of the major causes of highway deaths and injuries, accounting for about half of all annual (circa 50,000) motor vehicle fatalities.[19] Each year, drinking drivers (.01 or more) are involved in crashes that take the lives of 20,000-25,000 people (nearly seventy drinking-driving deaths a day), a figure that has not changed substantially in twenty-five years.[20] In 1988, for example, of the 47,093 people killed in traffic accidents, 23,352 were alcohol-related deaths (see Table 1.1), with most of the intoxicated parties having BALs well above .10.[21]

This means that in a typical two-year period, almost as many Americans die in drunk driving incidents as were killed on the battlefield during the entire ten-year Vietnam War.[22] In the past decade, a quarter of a million people have perished in alcohol-involved auto crashes, equivalent to the entire population of Rochester, New York.[23] The actual number and proportion of persons killed (and injured) by drinking drivers may be even higher, because almost one-third of the deceased drivers and 80 percent of surviving drivers are not tested for alcohol abuse.[24] In 1983, Texas tested just 2 percent of all fatally injured drivers, reflecting the low priority given to drunk driving in that state.[25]

Forty percent of the total (47,000) traffic fatalities occurred in crashes in which a driver or nonoccupant was legally drunk (.10

Table 1.1
Alcohol-Related Deaths, 1983-1988

Year	Deaths
1988	23,352
1987	23,632
1986	23,990
1985	22,360
1984	23,760
1983	23,650

Source: National Highway Traffic Safety Administration

Figure 1.2
Death by Accident

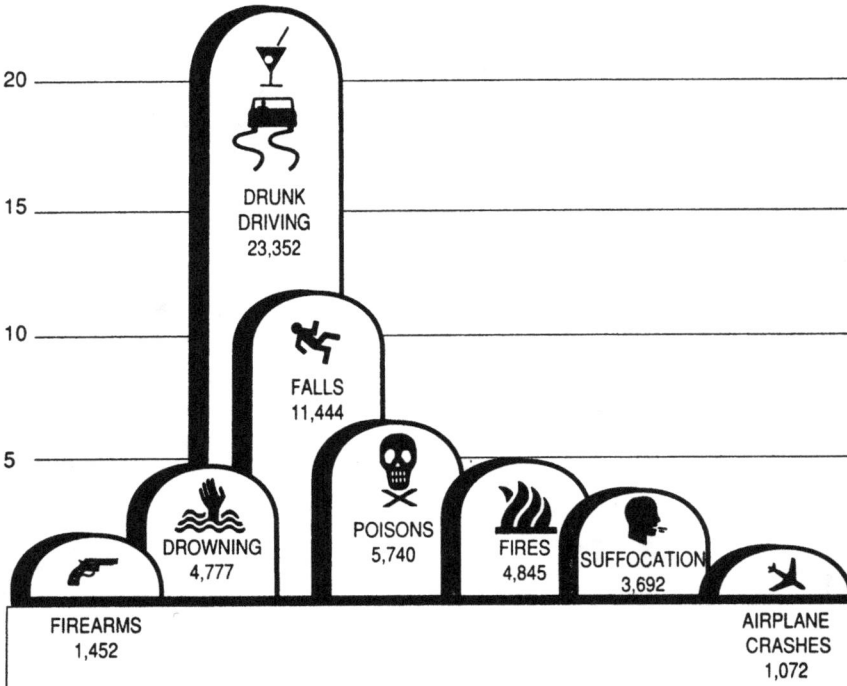

DRUNK DRIVING 23,352
FALLS 11,444
DROWNING 4,777
POISONS 5,740
FIRES 4,845
SUFFOCATION 3,692
FIREARMS 1,452
AIRPLANE CRASHES 1,072

BAC), and an additional 10 percent of the deaths involved individuals whose BAL was .01-.09, that is, who were in varying degrees functionally impaired.[26] Of the 18,500 people killed in drunk driving crashes, two-thirds were themselves intoxicated at the time.[27] The remaining victims were sober drivers, passengers, pedestrians, and pedacyclists. In addition, about 700,000 persons a year are injured—as many as 125,000 are permanently disabled or disfigured—in drunk driving crashes whose annual economic loss from property damage, medical costs, and related expenses is conservatively estimated at $21-24 billion.[28] Safety experts predict that one out of every two people will be involved in an alcohol-related crash at some point.[29]

The shocking reality is that, year in and year out, there are more alcohol-related traffic fatalities than there are murders, and that drunk drivers maim more innocent victims than all assaultive street criminals combined.[30] The lethal and often devastating consequences of mixing drinking and driving should make drunk driving eligible for inclusion in any list of serious and violent crimes.

2

Coming to Grips with Drunk Driving

OBSTACLES TO RECOGNIZING THE PROBLEM

Up until the early 1980s, society was reluctant to acknowledge that a drunk driving problem existed let alone to mount an aggressive counterattack against it. The public found it all too easy to identify with the offenders and to view them as decent law-abiding citizens (rather than criminals) caught up in a web of unfortunate circumstances over which they presumably had no control.[1] This "there but for the grace of God go I" attitude contributed to the criminal justice system's lethargic response to drunk driving cases, with courts and juries seemingly more concerned with giving drunk drivers a break and rehabilitation than with holding them accountable for their actions.[2]

Because of these policies and sentiments, diversion to treatment programs or DWI schools, wholesale plea bargaining, moralistic lectures, and no-jailtime sentences were the order of the day—even when victims were killed or seriously injured, or the drunk driver had a long record of prior DWI arrests and convictions. In 1981, for example, Idaho arrested 1,800 people for drunk driving, convicted one-third of them, and sent two to jail.[3] Legislators refused to support stricter drunk driving measures, reasoning that it was not in their personal self-interest to do so: "What if I'm at a party and have too much to drink and the cops stop me? Should the state be able to take away my license?"[4]

Social Acceptability of Drinking

A major obstacle to coming to grips with the problem is that the social acceptability of drinking is deeply ingrained in our culture, as evidenced by the repeal of Prohibition, an annual per-capita consumption of alcoholic beverages of 27.6 gallons (1985), and a $36 billion-per-year liquor industry. Drinking is not only big business but is also an integral part of doing business. And there are countless social situations and occasions in which drinking is not merely condoned but encouraged or expected. It is not surprising, then, that a majority of the population are at least social drinkers, that at one time or another most of us do drive after drinking, and that many people think little of having a couple of drinks at a gathering and then heading home with a final drink in hand.[5] For many men who regularly patronize neighborhood bars, drinking and driving is a kind of masculine rite of passage, a means of proving their cunning and machismo to themselves and their friends: "These workers spent as much time talking about how to blend alcohol and driving [and avoid detection] as they did discussing the Chicago Bears backfield."[6]

An Awakened Public

Because each activity separately (driving/drinking) is so closely integrated into the nation's social and economic fabric, the act of driving while intoxicated was almost immune from political critique and concerted reform until recently. Between 1980 and 1990, "few areas of law have received as much attention by legislatures, courts and the general public as the law governing the operation of motor vehicles while intoxicated."[7] The movement to expose drunk driving, to alter public attitudes, to revise the laws pertaining to Driving Under the Influence (DUI), and to change the justice system's response to the offenders began with the formation of Mothers Against Drunk Driving (MADD) in 1980 (see Close-up 2.1). Since then, the backlash against drunk drivers has evolved into a national moral crusade and multifaceted sociolegal agenda. Many of the now-standard countermeasures against drunk driving would have been unimaginable a few years ago were it not for the extraordinary efforts and accomplishments of MADD and the developments it led to.

Proliferation of Laws

In 1981 and 1982, forty-one states established task forces or commissions to examine the drunk driving problem and make recommendations for combating it.[8] Aided by the work of the Presidential Commission on Drunk Driving, these state efforts were the precusors to and formed the basis for subsequent new drunk driving statutes and amendments to DUI laws already on the books—the hallmark of which is deterrence and getting tough with offenders. Between 1982 and 1985 legislatures across the country introduced 3,000 proposals and passed 1,107 laws, running the gamut from comprehensive drunk driving packages to fine-tuning measures.[9] In 1987 alone, forty-five states passed some 216 new laws on the subject.[10] The main features of this punitive approach include a combination of civil and criminal sanctions discussed throughout this book.

ASAPs of 1970s

The federal government's first large-scale effort to control drunk driving occurred in the early 1970s, when the Department of Transportation invested over $88 million to fund experimental Alcohol Safety Action Programs (ASAPs) in thirty-five communities across the country. The thrust of this program was to increase apprehensions of drunk drivers and to provide increased counseling and education in order to prevent recidivism.[11] Evaluation of the ASAPs, however, failed to document even modest success for the program as a whole. For example, studies comparing arrested drivers who were offered treatment and education with drivers given standard penalties showed little difference in subsequent re-arrest rates and/or accident involvement.[12] Consequently, the projects were discontinued after federal funding ran out. Even if the results had been more encouraging, it is doubtful whether the project would have been retained or expanded, given the large expenditures involved and the general lack of public support for such endeavors at the time.

Close-up 2.1: Getting MADD and RID of Drunk Drivers

On May 3, 1980, thirteen-year old Cari Lightner was on her way to a church carnival in Fair Oaks (Calif.), walking inside the bicycle path, when a car swerved out of control, killed her, and sped away.

The driver, Clarence Busch, had a long record of DWI arrests, for which he had spent a grand total of *two days* behind bars.[a] Just the week before he killed Cari, Busch was released on bail in connection with another hit-and-run drunk driving charge. When a police officer told Candy Lightner that Busch would probably never serve time for killing her daughter, Candy quit her real estate job and launched Mothers Against Drunk Driving (MADD). In doing so, she provided the anti-drunk driving cause with what it needed most: a dedicated, determined, and outspoken constituency of victims and their relatives who molded public opinion and mobilized citizen support.[b] (The judge did not impose the maximum sentence on Busch for Cari's death because the court considered his alcoholism a mitigating factor. Busch was sent to a work camp and then to a halfway house, and was released after serving eleven months. In September 1985 Busch was convicted of injuring a girl in an auto accident and sentenced to four years in prison. It was his fourth conviction in six arrests for alcohol-related offenses.)

The circumstances under which the legal system's response to drunk drivers transforms the victim's grief into anger and then into action is, regrettably, an all too common one. The drunk at the wheel of a van that barrelled off a Massachusetts highway, pinning and killing fifteen-year old Paul Lawler, was on probation for his third conviction at the time. He was sentenced to four and one-half years in prison, making him eligible for parole just two years later. "I was under the impression anyone arrested for this kind of thing would have the book thrown at him," said Carol Lawler, Paul's mother who became the head of Greater Boston's MADD chapter. While witnessing the trial of the drunk driver (.26 BAC) who killed their fifteen-year old son, Thomas and Dorothy Sexton saw a car thief sentenced to two years in jail. After pleading guilty to vehicular homicide, their son's killer was given two years probation and fined $200, which caused the Sextons to become active in Maryland's MADD chapter.[c]

Because of dispositions like these, MADD had become the driving force behind the movement to reform drunk driving laws, to encourage societal intolerance of drunk drivers, and to alter the benign attitudes of prosecutors and judges toward the offense and the offenders.[d] Through its Texas-based national headquarters, its 1.1 million members, and 400 chapters in every state, MADD aggressively enunciates its agenda to legislatures, community and business groups, and other concerned citizens interested in doing something about the problem.[e] Although MADD has a counseling component to aid victims and their family members, MADD is much more than a self-help group. Based on an essentially punitive ideology, the bulk of MADD's activity is directed toward lobbying for various legislative changes—harsher penalties in particular—and compelling criminal justice practitioners to take drunk driving more seriously. In response to Lighter's unrelenting efforts, California passed a new law in 1981 imposing a mandatory prison term of up to four years for repeat offenders and minimum fines of $1375, the toughest state drunk driving law in the country at that time. At the federal level, MADD was instrumental in the creation of the Presidential Commission on Drunk Driving and passage of the 1984 national Minimum Drinking Age act.

One way of ensuring that available stiffer penalties are actually forthcoming is by bringing community pressure to bear on the courts at the sentencing stage. Through its Legal Advocacy program, MADD trains volunteers to serve as "court watchers" who monitor how prosecutors and judges handle impaired driving cases and evaluate the judicial proceedings.[f] The expectation is that judges will become more sensitive to the plight of victims, will order and give priority to Victim Impact Statements before sentencing, and will mete out sentences commensurate with the harm caused by convicted drunk drivers.[g] Because of MADD's courtwatching operation, defense lawyers who come before the North Carolina County District Traffic Court are now more inclined to advise their clients to plead guilty: "I don't think that I can get you off this time because that lady's sitting there listening."[h] Once drunk drivers have been taken out of circulation, MADD believes, there will be time and opportunity enough to provide for their treatment and rehabilitation—which have been conspicuously devalued as the principal dispostion under the deterrence model.

Remove Intoxicated Drivers (RID), created in 1978, has also played a pioneering role in the anti-drunk driving movement. Founded by Doris Aiken under similarly tragic circumstances, the New York based group has 25,000 members in 130 chapters in thirty-six states.[i] Its programs and goals are similar to MADD's, replete with victim hotlines and counseling, lobbying for change, victim witness panels, legislative vigils, outreach projects, and keeping tabs on how locally elected public officials vote on drunk driving measures and publishing the results. Its goals also "include actively curbing the alcoholizing of our environment." RID's two remaining top priorities are the immediate license suspension of arrested drunk drivers and more-widespread employment of sobriety checks.[j]

aBonnie Steinbock, "Drunk Driving," *Philosophy and Public Affairs* 14, no. 3 (1985): 279.

bTime, January 7, 1985, p. 41; *Newsweek,* September 13, 1982, p. 36.

c Ibid., *Newsweek.*

d Candy Lightner, "M.A.D.D. at the Court," *Judges Journal* (Spring 1984): 37.

e *USA Today,* March 9, 1989, p. 2D.

f MADD Victim Information pamphlet, p. 17.

g Alberta I. Cook, "A New Push on Drunken Drivers," *National Law Journal,* February 9, 1987, p. 8.

h *Newsweek,* September 13, 1982, p. 37.

i Paula Patyk, "The War Against Drunk Driving," *50 Plus* (May 1983), reprint, unnumbered pages.

j Ray McAllister, "The Drunken Driving Crackdown: Is It Working?" *ABA Journal,* September 1, 1988, p. 55.

BADD
Business Against Drunk Drivers, Inc.

After MADD got the ball rolling, various grass-roots efforts against drunk drivers proliferated. DADD, started in 1986, teaches drivers with mobile phones how to identify drunk drivers and promptly report them to the police. BADD, formed in 1987, opened a new front in the battle against drunk driving by mobilizing the resources, talent, and power of the business community to confront the problem.

DEVELOPMENTS DURING THE REAGAN ADMINISTRATION

Presidential Commission on Drunk Driving

The Presidential Commission on Drunk Driving, appointed by President Reagan in April 1982, was the culmination of a demand for White House action by MADD, RID, and an increasingly vociferous public. Reagan also signed legislation in 1982 encouraging the states to crack down on drunk drivers by making $75 million available to the states over the following three years as grant money for a variety of drunk driving control programs.[13]

After holding hearings in eight cities in the course of a year and thoroughly reviewing state and local programs, the commission made thirty-nine recommendations in its 1983 final report for alleviating the drunk driving problem in the United States, the most significant of which include the following:

• Increase the perceived risk of apprehension by having newspapers report the names and addresses of persons arrested and/or convicted of DUI.

• Establishments serving alcoholic beverages should display signs informing customers of the laws relating to alcohol use and highway safety. Commercial servers should receive special training for recognizing the signs of alcohol abuse and for identifying customers who are "visibly intoxicated."

• Enact "dram shop" laws establishing liability of any person who sells or serves alcoholic beverages to an individual who is visibly intoxicated.

• Prohibit the consumption of alcoholic beverages in motor vehicles through open-container laws.

• Employ selective police enforcement practices and other innovative techniques, including the use of judicially approved drunk driving roadblocks.

• Establish an implied-consent statute that provides that all drivers in that state are deemed to have given their consent to tests of blood, breath, or urine to determine their alcohol or drug concentration; and provide sufficiently severe license suspensions to discourage drivers from refusing the test.

Photo 2.1
John Volpe

John Volpe, former governor of Massachusetts, was the head of the thirty-member Presidential Commission on Drunk Driving. Drunk driving became a national priority in the Reagan administration, with the creation of the Presidential Commission in 1982. Many of the Presidential Commission's recommendations have been widely adopted and are discussed throughout this book. Photo courtesy of Governor John Volpe.

• Do not reduce DUI charges through plea bargaining.

• Enact legislation making it illegal per se for a person to be driving with a BAC of .10 or higher.

• Establish a system of mandatory punishments (involving license suspensions, fines and jail) calibrated to whether the convicted defendant was a first-time violator or repeat offender.

• Preconviction diversion to alcohol education or alcohol treatment programs should be eliminated. A finding on the charge should be rendered and participation in education or treatment programs should then become a condition of sentencing.

• Rehabilitation and education programs for individuals convicted of DUI should be provided as a supplement to other sanctions and not as a replacement for those sanctions.

• Any person convicted for DUI who causes personal injury or property damage should be required to make restitution.

• Courts should require victim impact statements (including oral or written statements by victims or survivors) prior to sentencing in all cases where death or serious injury results from a DUI offense.

The commission minced no words in criticizing the judiciary for failing to recognize and view drunk driving "as a serious offense meriting certain, swift and appropriate punishment." Among the commission's recommendations was a call for the formation of a permanent nongovernment organization to ensure a continuing focus on efforts to combat drunk driving and to carry out the commission's "blueprint for change." The National Commission Against Drunk Driving, established in 1984 in response to that proposal, is a nonprofit public service organization whose principal purpose is to assist the states, local governments, and the private sector in implementing the recommendations of the Presidential Commission.[14] Toward this end, the National Commission conducts research on the effectiveness of drunk driving countermeasures, serves as a national clearinghouse for innovative model programs and their dissemination, tracks the current status of anti-drunk driving laws and developments, and works closely with private industry and corporations to extend the anti-drunk driving message throughout the workplace.[15]

Surgeon General's Workshop on Drunk Driving

Under the leadership of then-surgeon general C. Everett Koop, a Workshop on Drunk Driving was held in Washington, D.C.,

Photo 2.2
National Commission Against Drunk Driving

The National Commission Against Drunk Driving is a private organization that assists and encourages the states, local governments, and the private sector in their efforts to combat drunk driving. Photo courtesy of the National Commission Against Drunk Driving.

December 14-16, 1988. The recommendations made by the surgeon general's panel of experts in the proceedings are in basic agreement with those of the Presidential Commission.[16] An underlying tenet of every group that has studied the problem is the need to change society's attitudes toward accepting, condoning, and tolerating drunk driving, that is, to make drunk driving socially unacceptable. In this regard the panel of experts went so far as to adopt a no-tolerance threshold (0.00 BAC) for persons under twenty-one as well as a nighttime driving curfew for this group.

A special concern and focus of the workshop was a set of recommendations designed to discourage the consumption and reduce the availability of alcohol through increasing the excise tax on alcoholic beverages, eliminating happy-hours, restricting alcohol sales by time and place at public events (such as sports events or concerts), and requiring that warning labels accompany all alcohol advertising to alert consumers to the various hazards of over-indulgence.[17] The most controversial proposal in this package was that certain types of advertising and marketing practices should be voluntarily restricted by the beverage producers themselves because

Table 2.1
National Commission for Drunk Driving Countermeasures

1988 NATIONAL COMMISSION AGAINST
Checklist of State Drunk Driving

	AL	AK	AZ	AR	CA	CO	CT	DE	FL	GA	HI	ID	IL	IN	IA	KS	KY	LA	ME	MD	MA	MI	MN	MS	MO	MT	NE	NV	NH	NJ	NM	NY
†1. administrative license suspension/revocation		•	•		•		•		•				•	•	•	•		•	•			•	•	•		•				•		
2. safety belt law				•	•	•		•	•	•	•	•	•	•	•	•		•		•		•	•		•	•		•		•	•	•
†3. open container law		•			•				•		•		•		•	•			•		•	•		•								
†4. dram shop statute	•	•	•			•	•		•	•		•	•	•	•		•		•		•	•	•	•	•			•	•	•	•	•
†5. .10 or lower per se level	•	•	•	•	•	•	•	•	•		•	•	•	•	•	•		•	•		•	•	•	•	•	•	•	•	•	•	•	•
†6. preliminary breath test permitted by law		•			•		•	•		•				•		•	•	•		•		•	•									
†7. BAC test refusal admitted admissible in court	•	•	•		•	•	•	•	•	•	•	•	•	•	•	•	•	•		•		•	•	•			•			•	•	
†8. greater license sanctions for DWI offenders under 21		•		•	•		•		•				•	•		•		•	•	•		•		•							•	•
†9. victim restitution	•	•		•	•	•	•	•	•	•	•	•	•	•	•	•	•	•	•		•	•	•	•	•			•			•	•
10. victim impact statement permitted		•	•	•	•		•	•		•		•	•	•	•		•		•		•		•					•	•	•		
†11. user funded programs		•	•	•	•		•	•			•	•	•	•		•		•	•	•							•	•	•		
†12. DUI plea bargaining prohibited	•		•	•	•	•			•				•	•								•			•			•		•		
13. DWI-related death considered a felony	•		•	•	•	•	•	•	•	•	•	•	•	•	•	•		•	•		•		•	•	•	•	•	•			•	•
†14. mandatory alcohol evaluation		•	•	•	•		•		•		•	•	•		•	•				•	•	•			•				•			
†15. mandatory 90-day loss of license for 1st offense DWI	•	•	•			•	•	•		•		•	•		•	•		•	•		•								•	•	•	•
16. Exchange information on DWI convictions with other state	•	•	•	•	•	•	•	•	•	•	•	•	•	•	•	•	•	•	•	•	•	•	•	•	•	•	•	•	•	•	•	•
17. mandatory jail for driving on on suspended/revoked license	•	•	•	•	•	•	•	•		•	•	•	•	•		•			•		•				•				•	•	•	•
18. mandatory training for all alcohol servers/clerks				•																												
19. two or more DWI questions on license examination	•	•	•	•	•	•	•	•	•	•	•	•	•	•	•	•	•	•	•		•	•	•	•		•	•	•	•	•	•	•

The District of Columbia has 11 of the 19 countermeasures. They are numbers 1,2,5,7,10,11,13,14,15,16 and 19.

† = denotes Alcohol Traffic Safety Incentive Grant Funds 23 U.S.C. 408.

* = denotes 21 states which have qualified for 408 funds.

L1860-7

16

DRUNK DRIVING
Countermeasures

N. CAROLINA	N. DAKOTA*	OHIO	OKLAHOMA*	OREGON*	PENNSYLVANIA	RHODE ISLAND*	S. CAROLINA	S. DAKOTA	TENNESSEE	TEXAS*	UTAH*	VERMONT	VIRGINIA	WASHINGTON*	W. VIRGINIA*	WISCONSIN	WYOMING	YES	NO
•	•		•	•							•			•	•	•		23	27
•		•	•		•			•	•	•		•	•		•			31	19
•	•		•	•			•	•			•			•		•		20	30
•	•	•		•	•	•				•	•	•	•			•	•	34	16
•	•	•	•	•	•	•	•	•	•	•	•	•	•			•	•	43	7
•	•				•	•		•				•	•		•			25	25
•	•	•	•	•	•	•	•	•	•	•	•	•	•		•	•	•	44	6
•			•			•				•					•	•		21	29
•	•	•	•	•	•	•	•	•	•	•	•	•	•		•	•	•	44	6
•				•		•	•					•	•					24	26
•	•		•	•	•	•	•	•	•	•	•	•	•	•	•	•		40	10
•				•	•							•					•	18	32
•		•		•	•	•	•	•	•	•	•		•	•	•	•	•	39	11
•	•		•	•	•	•			•	•		•			•			25	25
	•		•	•	•	•			•	•		•			•	•		29	21
•	•	•	•	•	•	•	•	•	•	•	•	•	•	•	•	•	•	49	1
	•				•	•	•		•				•		•			25	25
			•	•							•							4	46
•	•		•	•	•	•	•	•	•	•	•	•	•	•	•	•	•	46	4

Survey reflects legislation passed as of October 1, 1988.

Countermeasure Definitions

1. Pre-conviction license suspension or revocation for all drivers whose Blood Alcohol Content (BAC) exceeds the legal limit or who refuse to take a BAC test.
2. Safety belts required by law for drivers of all ages.
3. Open container law prohibiting all unsealed alcohol beverage containers in passenger compartment of motor vehicle for all occupants of all ages.
4. Dram shop statute which makes those who dispense alcoholic beverages to intoxicated individuals liable for subsequent injuries caused by such individuals.
5. Illegal per se law making it an offense to operate a motor vehicle with a BAC of .10% or higher.
6. Preliminary Breath Test specifically permitted by law.
7. A driver's refusal to be chemically tested for alcohol is permitted by law to be introduced as evidence of guilt in a court trial for DWI.
8. State law provides for greater license sanctions for DWI offenders under age 21.
9. A driver convicted of causing personal injury or damage while driving impaired can be ordered by a judge to pay restitution to the victim and/or to the victim's family.
10. Victims and/or their families have a statutory right to make a victim impact statement prior to sentencing in DWI cases involving death or serious injury.
11. Convicted drunk drivers are required to pay for the cost of the rehabilitative activities or treatment to which they are sentenced.
12. Plea bargaining is prohibited by statute in all DWI cases.
13. State law makes it an automatic felony for a DWI driver to kill a person in a motor vehicle crash.
14. Convicted DWI offenders are required by law to undergo a pre-sentence or post-sentence evaluation for alcohol problems.
15. First offense DWI is punishable by a mandatory 90-day license suspension or revocation. In keeping with the 408 criteria, states can meet this by having a 30-day hard suspension followed by a 60-day restricted suspension.
16. State exchanges information on DWI convictions with other states. While 49 states reported exchanging information on DWI convictions with other states, only 40 states reported exchanging information on implied consent refusals.
17. State law establishes a mandatory jail sentence for anyone convicted of driving on a license that was suspended or revoked because of a DWI offense.
18. State law requires mandatory training for all liquor licensees and all retail servers and sales clerks.
19. State driver's license examination includes two or more questions specifically designed to determine the applicant's knowledge of the relationship of alcohol and other drugs to highway safety.

Photo 2.3
Beer Institute Advertisement

DRUNK DRIVING IS ONE PROBLEM THE BREWERS ARE FACING HEAD ON.

One sure way to get drunk drivers off the road is to hire a cab for them. So we do. Alert Cab is a program that offers a free or reduced

taxi ride to anyone who is unable to drive safely home from a bar or restaurant. The bartender has a confidential telephone number to

call when summoning a cab. Alert Cab, though, is just one way to keep drunk drivers off the road. We also support "Designated Driver"

programs such as I'm Driving. And we've developed Think When You Drink, a television campaign that urges people to not drive drunk.

The Beer Institute is also active at the community level. A.D.D.Y. —Alcohol, Drugs, Driving and You—educates teenagers on how drugs

and alcohol affect judgment and driving performance. And our Community Assistance Fund provides money directly for education and

prevention programs. ☐ None of these programs, however, is designed to take the place of responsible drinking. To learn more about everything

we're doing to address the problem of alcohol abuse write James C. Sanders, President of the Beer Institute, 1225 Eye Street, NW, Suite 825,

Washington, D.C. 20005. ☐ We're doing something about the problem of alcohol abuse. With your help we can find a solution together.

BEER INSTITUTE

The Beer Institute is the trade association for American brewers and their suppliers. It is dedicated to responsible consumption of their fine quality beers.

The Beer Institute advertisement and a realistic portrayal of the consequences of drinking and driving by the media were the kinds of "counter messages" urged by the Surgeon General's Panel of Experts. Photo courtesy of the Beer Institute.

such practices "clearly send the wrong messages about alcohol consumption to the wrong audiences. These practices tell youth that alcohol consumption leads to athletic, social and sexual success. They send the messages that drinking is a normal and glamorous activity without negative consequences, and our young people are believing those messages.[18]

Although the workshop indicated that it was not calling for a ban on alcohol advertisements, the perception in some quarters was that the surgeon general was out to get the $2 billion-a-year alcohol advertising industry, even if it meant infringing on their right to free speech and the principles of free enterprise. In actuality, the panel of experts was urging the alcoholic beverage industry and mass media to make a concerted effort to project pro-health and pro-safety messages in their promotional activities and programming. "We're not talking about banning advertising. We're talking about evening it out so that the public health consequences of this problem, which are massive in our society, can be told."[19] These "counter ads" advocated by the workshop, portraying the dangers of drinking and driving for example, were deemed necessary in order to counteract alcohol commercials dominating the airways targeted to impressionable teenage drinkers and depicting alcoholic beverages "as if they were as wholesome as skim milk."[20] The kind of innovative counter ads envisaged by the workshop are illustrated by commercials such as "Know When To Say When," sponsored by Anheuser Busch, and by utilizing television programs—which typically portray characters who drink too much and drive too fast as "cool" role models—to have an impact on social norms relating to drunk driving.

3

The Police Response to Drunk Drivers

STOPPING DRIVERS FOR CAUSE

Reasonable Suspicion

The usual way drunk drivers are identified and apprehended is when a police officer (on roving patrol) stops a motorist for some type of suspicious, erratic, improper, unusual, or illegal driving behavior. Any of the conditions in Exhibit 3.1, which may indicate alcohol impairment, provide the officer with *reasonable suspicion* for stopping a vehicle. Reasonable suspicion is the legal standard (quantum of evidence) needed to warrant police officers' stopping and detaining motorists on their own discretion. Reasonable suspicion means there is reason to suspect (a reasonable possibility)—which can be objectively articulated—that the driver or other occupant has committed, is committing, or is about to commit a crime.[1]

Reasonable suspicion car stops and the subsequent brief detention entailed do not violate the Fourth Amendment prohibition against unreasonable seizures because the warrantless seizure (the stop) is reasonable. The purpose of the stop is, through further investigation, to get additional information that will either confirm or dispel the officer's suspicion of criminal conduct. There is virtually no limit to

Exhibit 3.1
Possible Indicators of Alcohol Impairment That Provide Reasonable Suspicion To Stop Motorist

---

- making wide turns
- weaving in roadway
- straddling/riding center line
- nearly striking another vehicle
- following too closely
- driving on wrong side of road
- speeding/driving very slowly
- braking erratically
- turning abruptly or illegally
- stopping inappropriately in driving lane
- drifting from lane to lane
- driving on non-designated surfaces
- signalling inconsistently
- slow response time to traffic lights
- having headlights off at night

Based on: "Jefferson County Drunk Busters," *FBI Law Enforcement Bulletin,* June
    1989, p. 20.

the range of motorist behavior that may give rise to reasonable suspicion. In essence, the police have reasonable suspicion to stop and detain a motorist (or pedestrian) whenever doing so would be deemed judicially appropriate in view of the circumstances and facts leading up to and immediately preceding such action.

Probable Cause

Although reasonable suspicion authorizes the officer to take certain investigative steps after the initial stop, it is insufficient for making an arrest. The police must have probable cause to arrest for any crime. Probable cause to arrest means there are reasonable grounds to believe or conclude that a crime has been committed and the person in question committed it. In other words, there must be a substantial probability of the suspect's guilt.[2] Probable cause exists if all the data, the combination of facts, factors, observations, and information available to the officer, would lead a reasonably cautious or reasonably prudent individual to conclude that the

Figure 3.1
Legal Standards of Proof for Decision Making

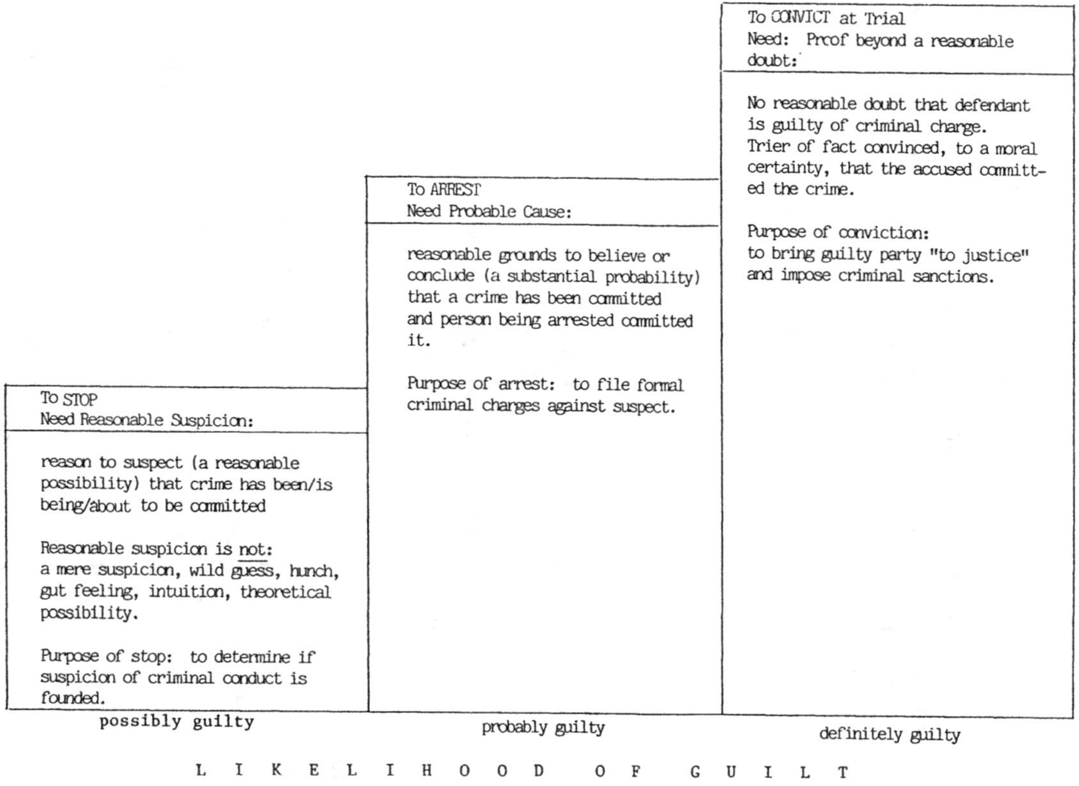

To STOP
Need Reasonable Suspicion:

reason to suspect (a reasonable possibility) that crime has been/is being/about to be committed

Reasonable suspicion is not: a mere suspicion, wild guess, hunch, gut feeling, intuition, theoretical possibility.

Purpose of stop: to determine if suspicion of criminal conduct is founded.

To ARREST
Need Probable Cause:

reasonable grounds to believe or conclude (a substantial probability) that a crime has been committed and person being arrested committed it.

Purpose of arrest: to file formal criminal charges against suspect.

To CONVICT at Trial
Need: Proof beyond a reasonable doubt:

No reasonable doubt that defendant is guilty of criminal charge. Trier of fact convinced, to a moral certainty, that the accused committed the crime.

Purpose of conviction: to bring guilty party "to justice" and impose criminal sanctions.

possibly guilty   probably guilty   definitely guilty

L I K E L I H O O D O F G U I L T

subject is probably guilty of the crime for which he is being arrested.[3] After a car has been stopped for reasonable suspicion, how do the police decide if the driver is legally intoxicated, that is, if there is probable cause for a DWI arrest?

Making DWI Arrest Decision

The development of probable cause begins when the officer approaches the car, asks to see a driver's license and registration card, and inquires about the erratic driving—all the while sizing up the motorist for possible cues of drunkenness. ("Do you know why I stopped you? Were you aware that you were crossing the center line?") Police observation of the outward signs (indicia) of intoxication include such things as:

- the driver's appearance and general demeanor,
- the smell of alcohol (was it faint, or was the driver reeking of alcohol?),
- slurred or incoherent speech,
- watery, bloodshot eyes or a flushed face,
- fumbling while locating or producing identification,
- an alcoholic beverage in plain sight,
- responses to questions concerning recent or excessive consumption of alcohol.

If there are *no* indicia of DWI (or other crimes) at this stage, then the reasonable suspicion that triggered the stop has been dispelled, there are no grounds for asking the driver to perform field sobriety tests, and the officer must allow the driver to go.[4]

On the other hand, the presence of one or more of the above indicia of intoxication would verify the officer's reasonable suspicion and justify asking the driver to consent to roadside sobriety tests. Should the motorist refuse to cooperate, the officer must assess whether the circumstances up to that point would constitute probable cause for a DWI arrest. The smell of alcohol alone, with nothing more to go on, would generally not amount to probable cause, and the officer would have to discontinue the detention. (There may be probable cause to arrest for some other crime or for the original traffic violation, if they are arrestable offenses.) But an odor of alcohol along with other indicia of intoxication, coupled with the reasons for stopping the car in the first place, would normally be sufficient to establish probable cause. Moreover, in some jurisdic-

Photo 3.1
MADD Official with Minnesota State Trooper

Sharon Gerhman, head of the Hennipin County MADD chapter, often rides along, as an observer, with the Minnesota State Police on Labor Day weekends and other holidays. Gerhman keeps a log of every person arrested for drunk driving and checks the police records to find out if the driver is a repeater. Gerhman or another MADD member will follow up the case to see what happens to the offender, a process that may include assigning a court-watcher to the trial and sentencing stage. "Before MADD started, drinking and driving was a socially accepted form of homicide. The law enforcement [community] will tell you that. It is no longer socially accepted, and we must let the public know, as the system does, that no one will tolerate it any more." Photo courtesy of Sharon Gerhman, Chapter Administrator, Hennipin County Chapter of MADD.

tions the driver's refusal to consent to field sobriety tests is itself a factor that may contribute to the formation or probable cause, the refusal implying guilty knowledge on the part of the uncooperative suspect.[5] Even though "good" DWI arrests may be made without field sobriety tests, police usually prefer to have the field test results in order to be on the safe side and to lay the foundation for a successful DWI prosecution and conviction. In practice, of course, most drivers routinely consent to the field sobriety tests.

FIELD SOBRIETY TESTS

Historically, roadside sobriety tests (see Exhibit 3.2) used by police to make DWI arrests and to build cases that would stand up in court varied widely, were administered in a nonuniform fashion, and ultimately depended on the officer's subjective evaluation of the driver's motor coordination skills.[6] Poor performance might be due to any number of reasons other than intoxication, such as medical

Exhibit 3.2
Field Sobriety Tests

Field (or roadside) sobriety tests are simple tests of motor coordination used to aid police officers in determining if there is sufficient (probable) cause to make a drunk driving arrest. The most commonly used roadside sobriety tests include:

1. the Rhomberg Balance test. The diver stands straight while the officer looks for swaying, stumbling, falling, or need for support.

2. the walk-the-line test, also referred to as the walk-and-turn or heel-to-toe test. The driver is asked to walk a straight line by putting one foot directly in front of the other. The officer attends to any loss of balance, especially when the driver is turning.

3. the finger-to-nose or touch-your-nose test. With heels together and arms extended to each side, the driver is instructed to touch his nose with the tips of his index fingers. This test checks the driver's peripheral vision and hand-eye coordination.

4. the alphabet test. Driver is asked to recite the alphabet slowly. Officer detects any loss of concentration that is signaled by not remembering what letter comes next.

---

problems, the driver's age, educational and cultural factors, where and when the tests were conducted, among others. The validity of prefield test indicia of intoxication was likely to be discredited at trial by defense counsel: "Don't most cars *weave* on the highway?" And without knowing how the driver ordinarily sounds, how credible is the officer's testimony concerning a driver's "slurred speech"?[7] Consequently, police officers were often hard pressed to substantiate the in-car or field test observations and conclusions on which a DWI arrest decision was made, thereby weakening the chances for conviction.

Gaze-Nystagmus Test

In 1977 the National Highway Traffic Safety Administration (NHTSA) contracted with the Southern California Research Institute to identify the most accurate field tests for determining alcohol impairment. After evaluating a variety of commonly used sobriety techniques under controlled conditions, the institute concluded that three tests,when administered in a standardized fashion, were highly reliable indicators of alcohol impairment: the walk-and-turn test, the one-leg stand test, and most important, the *gaze-nystagmus* test. The gaze test was considered the most sensitive preliminary sobriety test that can conveniently[8] be administered at roadside.[9] A police officer simply moves a pen or other such object in front of the suspect's face in a horizontal manner. A sober person's eyes will smoothly follow the motion of the pen, but an intoxicated person's eyes will involuntarily jerk or balance abruptly. This "nystagmus" (involuntary jerking) may be the first clue to identifying motorists with a .10 BAC. In the case of someone who is drunk, "the farther the eye moves, the more the jerking is exaggerated by alcohol."[10] Besides being involuntary, the nystagmus reaction is completely unconscious, so that the subject is not aware it is happening and is powerless to control it.

The initial 1977 study found that officers trained to use gaze nystagmus were able to determine if the suspect's BAC was .10 in 77 percent of the cases. A subsequent validation of the gaze test by NHTSA researchers in 1981, based on 1,500 cases in four states, "confirmed that horizontal gaze nystagmus is the most reliable roadside test available to police officers for establishing probable cause for arrest." On the average, police were able to accurately judge BACs above and below .10 in 82 percent of the cases, compared to

Photo 3.2
Officer Administering Gaze-Nystagmus Test

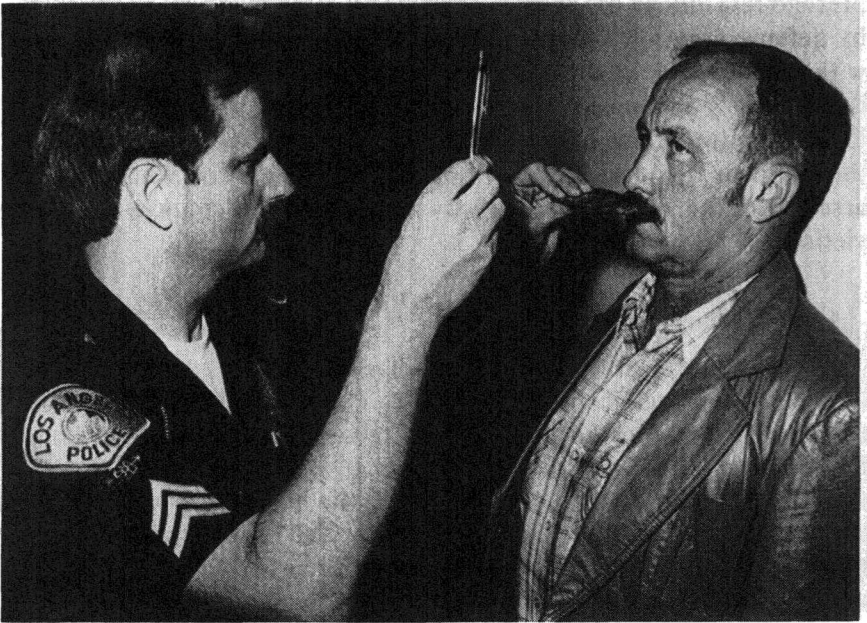

A Los Angeles police officer demonstrating the horizontal *gaze-nystagmus* (eye) test, an involuntary jerking of the eyeball as it follows the motion of an object, such as a pen. Studies show that by using gaze nystagmus, police are able to identify drivers with a .10 BAC or over with a high degree of accuracy. Photo courtesy of Sgt. Richard Stoddard/L.A.P.D.

the 20 to 30 percent accuracy level associated with many other roadside sobriety testing procedures.[11] The nystagmus test has not only proven to be far superior to the other nonchemical roadside tests but also has the added advantage of allowing an officer the chance to spot "a drunk who's practiced at masking the symptoms of insobriety because he's living life drunk." Gaze-nystagmus results cannot be used in court to prove a specific, numerical BAC; for example, they cannot be used as a substitute for chemical intoxication tests. However, the Arizona Supreme Court has held that gaze nystagmus is a valid scientific principle under the *Frye* test and, hence, is admissible evidence at trial bearing on the defendant's guilt or innocence.[12]

4
Sobriety Checkpoints

I find this kind of Gestapo-like invasion of privacy intolerable. Don't write to me about the innocent people who are killed by drunken drivers . . . I mourn for the parents of children who have died at the hands of drunken drivers. But none of this makes a police state acceptable.[1]

STOPPING MOTORISTS WITHOUT REASONABLE SUSPICION

For quite some time, police departments in many states have used "sobriety checkpoints" as part of their overall DWI enforcement strategy. Under these programs, roadblocks are set up at certain locations, where all or some drivers are stopped for a cursory determination of alcohol impairment. The driver is allowed to proceed and may be given a traffic safety brochure for good measure if there are no obvious signs of intoxication. If there are, the scenario that follows is the same as when police stop drivers for cause. Sobriety checkpoint stops are seizures within the meaning of the Fourth Amendment. Therefore, the main legal issue was whether the initial roadblock stop of all vehicles or every nth car—which is not based on particularized (reasonable) suspicion—violates the Fourth Amendment safeguard against unreasonable seizure.

Legal Guidelines for Stops

The principles derived from a series of pre-1990 Supreme Court cases involving investigatory stops were as follows (see Table 4.1). Police officers who rely on their own discretion to stop a citizen must have *individualized suspicion* before doing so; particularized suspicion is a prerequisite for discretionary stops. On the other hand, investigatory stops may be made without reasonable suspicion when police discretion in deciding who shall be stopped is eliminated or controlled, and when, all things considered, the public interest in conducting such stops takes priority over the individual's right to "personal security from arbitrary interference by law officers."[2] The latter guideline refers to the *balancing test* enunciated by the Supreme Court in *Brown* v. *Texas* and provides the key for determing whether suspicionless stops are reasonable or unreasonable seizures.

Balancing Test

In *Brown* the Court declared that the constitutionality of investigatory stops involves "a weighing of the gravity of the public concerns served by the seizure, the degree to which the seizure advances the public interest, and the severity of the interference with individual liberty." In an earlier decision, the Court approved the Border Patrol's routine stopping of all vehicles at a stationary checkpoint because "the government or public interest in making such stops [stemming illegal immigration] outweighs the constitutionally protected interest of the private citizen," and because the immigration checkpoints involved minimal discretionary enforcement activity: "Since field officers may stop only those cars passing the checkpoint, there is less room for abusive or harassing stops of individuals than there [is] in the case of roving-patrol stops." Utilizing the balancing test and quantum of police discretion, the courts have upheld suspicionless stops and limited searches in a variety of checkpoint-type settings: stopping outbound airplane passengers and inspecting their luggage with metal detectors, using roadblocks to apprehend escaped convicts, and examining persons entering places, (courtrooms or prisons, for instance) that pose special security risks, for example. These practices do not violate the Fourth

Table 4.1
Cases Illustrating When Police May Make Investigative Stops

Case	Description	Salient Factors In Decision	Fourth Amendment Violated?
Terry v. Ohio[a] (1968)	Officer observed two men repeatedly peering into store window, leaving, then returning to same store. Suspected they were casing store for a robbery and might be armed. When officer stopped men and got evasive reply to request for identification, officer frisked (a "search") Terry and discovered a gun.	Officer acting on own discretion. Had right to make stop because there was reasonable suspicion that criminal activity was afoot. Limited search of outer clothing (the "frisk") was permissible because there was reasonable suspicion subjects were armed and dangerous.	No
U.S. v. Brignoni-Ponce[b] (1975)	Officers on roving patrol near Mexican border stopped car to question occupants about their citizenship status. Singled out car solely because the occupants appeared to be of Mexican descent.	Roving patrol. Discretionary stop. Lacked reasonable suspicion for stop.	Yes
U.S. v. Martinez-Fuerte[c] (1976)	Border Patrol stopped all vehicles at inland checkpoint location known to be common route for smuggling aliens into country. Upon being directed to secondary area, two female passengers admitted they entered country unlawfully.	Checkpoint operation stops involve less police discretion than do roving-patrol stops (police discretion is controlled). The intrusion on one's freedom was quite limited, being restricted to the stop itself, being restricted to the stop itself, being questioning, and visual inspection. Such stops do not require individualized suspicion.	No
Delaware v. Prouse[d] (1979)	Officer on roving patrol stopped a car to check the driver's license and registration, without observing any traffic violation or suspicious activity of any kind. Officer observed marijuana in plain view on car floor, for which the driver was subsequently indicted.	Officer on roving patrol. Wholly discretionary, random (arbitrary) stop. Need articulable suspicion of wrongdoing before stopping car for license/registration check.	Yes

Table 4.1 *(continued)*

Case	Description	Salient Factors In Decision	Fourth Amendment Violated?
Brown v. Texas [e] (1979)	While cruising in patrol car, officer observed Brown and another man walking away from each other in an alley in an area with a high incidence of drug traffic. Officer stopped Brown, asked him to identify himself and explain what he was doing there, which Brown steadfastly refused to do and for which he was arrested. The officers had no reason to suspect Brown of any misconduct or that he was armed.	Roving Patrol. Discretionary stop. Need reasonable suspicion to justify stop for identification purpose. Merely being in neighborhood frequented by drug users does not amount to reasonable suspicion. Balance between government interest (crime prevention) in allowing random identification-stops and the citizen's right to be free from police interference tilts toward the latter.	Yes
Reid v. Georgia [f] (1980)	Upon arriving at the Atlanta airport, Reid and a companion were stopped by federal agents, who asked for identification and to see their tickets. The pair was stopped because they fit the "Drug Courier Profile" (DCP) used to identify passengers suspected of trafficking in narcotics. Cocaine was found in Reid's bag following the stop.	It was not a checkpoint-type operation, since only certain incoming passengers were singled out for a stop and detention. Although discretion was controlled, the DCP used was not considered a valid basis for establishing reasonable suspicion to stop passengers.	Yes

[a] *Terry v. Ohio*, 392 U.S. 1 (1968)
[b] *U.S. v. Brignoni-Ponce*, 422 U.S. 873 (1975)
[c] *U.S. v. Martinez-Fuerte*, 428 U.S. 543 (1976)
[d] *Delaware v. Prouse*, 440 U.S. 648 (1979)
[e] *Brown v. Texas*, 443 U.S. 47 (1979)
[f] *Reid v. Georgia*, No. 79-448. Decided June 30, 1980

Figure 4.1
Scales of Justice

The balancing test involves weighing the particular government interest (or societal objective) served by a particular law enforcement practice against the degree to which such official actions might infringe on one's constitutional rights—and deciding on balance which concerns should be given priority. The state interest always refers to some aspect of controlling crime and bringing offenders to justice, be it the generic goal of preventing crime or the more specific government interest in curtailing drunk driving. As applied to sobriety checkpoints, this balancing test requires an evaluation of how serious a problem drunk driving actually is and, hence, the state's interest in controlling it; the decision by authorities that such roadblocks advance the public interest involved; and how much the checkpoint stops and associated police activities interfere with a citizen's reasonable expectation of privacy. Reasonable minds, of course, may reach different conclusions when applying the balancing test.

Amendment because the scales of justice clearly tilt toward the public interest, police discretion is controlled, the intrusion on personal liberties is minimal, and there are no other less-intrusive alternatives for achieving the state's objective.

Delaware v. Prouse (1979)

The first indication by the Supreme Court that sobriety checkpoints might pass constitutional muster came, oddly enough, in a 1979 decision that required particularized suspicion whenever police single out motorists for a discretionary stop. A Delaware police officer on roving partol stopped a car at random to check the motorist's driver's license and vehicle registration. The officer saw a bag of marijuana in plain view on the car floor, seized it, and Prouse was subsequently indicted for illegal possession of a controlled substance. At a pretrial suppression hearing, the officer admitted that prior to stopping the vehicle he had no reason to suspect that the stopped motorist had or was about to break the law: "I saw the car in the area and was not answering any complaints so I decided to pull it off."[3] In its main holding, the Court ruled that because the officer did not have "specific articulable facts" that would amount to a reasonable suspicion that something was amiss, stopping Prouse for a document check was an unreasonable seizure. The Court's principal concern in Prouse, echoed in all the cases in Table 4.1, was the "grave danger" of the abuse of discretion inherent in "standardless and unconstrained discretion," potential abuses that reasonable suspicion would serve to curtail. Almost as a postscript to its main holding, the Court concluded its decision with, "This holding does not preclude the State of Delaware or other States from developing methods for spot checks that involve less intrusion or that do not involve the unconstitutional exercise of discretion. *Questioning of all oncoming traffic at roadblock-type stops is one possible alternative*" [emphasis mine].

This *Prouse* dicta was taken as a signal by many police departments and states that vehicles could be stopped without reasonable suspicion provided that the discretionary random stops were replaced with a systematic, strictly controlled alternative method, for example, the kind of discretionless stops made in sobriety checkpoints (see Exhibit 4.1).[4] The *Prouse* addendum seemed to imply that stopping cars on "neutral criteria" (all cars, every nth one), rather than unfettered police discretion, obviated the need for particularized suspicion and that such stops qualified as reasonable seizures for Fourth Amendment purposes.[5]

STATE COURT DECISIONS IN AFTERMATH OF PROUSE

Following *Prouse,* state court decisions concerning sobriety checkpoints fell into one of three categories (consult Table 4.2).

First, a minority of state courts invalidated drunk driving roadblocks solely because their state constitutions afford citizens greater protection (*more* due process) against unreasonable search and seizure than the Fourth Amendment, thereby flatly prohibiting the police from stopping anyone without individualized reasonable

Exhibit 4.1
Factors That Enhance Judicial Approval of Sobriety Checkpoints

1. Operational aspects of checkpoint must be determined by preexisting guidelines (a prior plan) established by police administrators, which field officers must follow to the letter.

2. Selection of checkpoint sites and times of operation must be made by supervisory officers who should be prepared to justify why those locations were chosen.

3. The public should be given advance notice, through local media publicity, of the times and locations of the checkpoint sites.

4. The stops must be limited in scope and duration. The guidelines should instruct field officers on such matters as how long drivers may be detained if nothing is wrong, how far officers may go in questioning drivers and observing the manifest signs of intoxication (can they shine flashlights inside car?), what action field officers can take, if any, if an approaching car makes a legal U-turn or turns off the road to avoid the stop.

5. Each car must have an equal chance of being stopped in order to assure that the stop is nondiscretionary and nondiscriminatory.

6. Checkpoints must be operated in a manner that ensures motorist safety, e.g., avoiding lengthy backups, assessing weather conditions, and having safe secondary areas, among others. If any condition jeapordizes safety, the checkpoint operation should be suspended.

7. Motorists approaching checkpoints must be warned in advance that they are subject to being stopped in order to allay fear and anxiety generated by the stop. Warning devices should include signs announcing the checkpoint, cones, and blinking lights, as well as a brief statement to each driver explaining why cars are being stopped.

Source: Lance J. Rogers, "The Drunk-Driving Roadblock," *Criminal Law Bulletin* (May-June 1985): 204; American Bar Association, *Drunk Driving Laws and Enforcement,* (February 1986): 4; Jerome O. Campane, "The Constitutionality of Drunk Driver Roadblocks, *FBI Law Enforcement Bulletin* (July 1984): 29.

Table 4.2

State Court Decisions on Sobriety Checkpoints in the Aftermath of *Prouse*

Decisions upholding Checkpoints	Salient Factors in Decision	Decisions Striking Down Checkpoints	Salient Factors in Decision
New Jersey Superior Court[a] (1980)	Written policy required safely stopping every fifth vehicle early in morning when nearby bars and tavern were closing. Roadblocks were located on a dangerous thoroughfare where several alcohol-related fatalities had occurred in previous two years. Flares were appropriately positioned to alert drivers and precautions taken to minimize anxiety over being stopped. Checkpoints most effective when stationed late at night along roads near dram shops.	Arizona Supreme Court[d] (1983)	Record disclosed no information on extent of drunk driving problem on Arizona highways. Motorists were taken by surprise, with no warning signs announcing purpose of stop nor prior notice of checkpoint locations through media publicity. Police not instructed where roadblocks were to be set up, whether to shine flashlight in cars, what to do if vehicle made U-turn.
Kansas Supreme Court[b] (1983)	Roadblock established in well-lit area whose location was selected by supervisory personnel. All vehicles in both directions were stopped. Sufficient field officers present to ensure that detention was minimal. High police visibility and flashing lights eased driver fears. First state supreme court to uphold reasonableness of DWI roadblock and to identify factors for assessing their legality.	Nebraska Supreme Court[e] (1986)	Acting on their own authority, Omaha patrol officers stopped every fourth vehicle on pretext of checking operator's documents, when the actual purpose was to detect drunk drivers. "A six or seven person unit within the department, commanded by a field sergeant, was free to decide when, where, and how to establish the transitory checkpoint."

| Massachusetts Supreme Court[c] (1985) | Roadblock operation conformed to established guidelines. Motorists given advance warning through news media. Police instructed to limit contact to one minute per car. Balance-of-interest test rendered checkpoint stops as reasonable seizure. |
| Pennsylvania Supreme Court[f] (1988) | Invalidated roadblocks in York and Delaware Counties, after taking notice of studies indicating that road-blocks could lead to apprehending only 1 out of every 2,000 drunk drivers estimated to be on the road. Not effective enough to justify intruding on privacy rights of so many sober drivers. |

[a]State v. Cocoomo, 427 A.2D 131 (N.J. Super. Ct. 1980)

[b]State v. Deskins, 673 P.2d 1174 (Kan. 1983)

[c]Massachusetts v. Trumble, October 15, 1985, 483 N.E.2d 1102

[d]State Ex Rel. Ekstrom v. Justice Ct. of State, 663 P.2d 992, 99 (Ariz. 1983)

[e]Neb. Sup Ct; State v. Crom, No. 84-471, 3/21/86, in 54 Law Week 2521-2522

[f]Insight, February 1, 1988, p. 54

suspicion. "The Oregon Constitution prohibits such indiscriminate police invasion of personal liberties [by means of sobriety checkpoints].[6]

Second, courts in sixteen states upheld roadblocks primarily because the checkpoints satisfied (almost) all of the conditions in Exhibit 4.1, the control of "unfettered discretion" being the sine qua non for judicial approval.[7] It was also the implicit or express opinion of these courts that the balancing test favored the state interest: the momentary, minimal intrusion on motorists' privacy was a minor inconvenience outweighed by "the magnitude of the drunk driving menace and the potential for deterrence."[8] Hence, "the State's action must be considered as a reasonable infringement upon the motorist's expectation of privacy."[9] Even though citizens are stopped without reasonable suspicion, sobriety checkpoints are not "dragnets whose purpose is an old-fashioned criminal investigation."[10]

Conversely, a number of courts invalidated roadblocks primarily because field officers were given too much operational leeway and/or because of some other defect in implementation. While approving the concept of sobriety checkpoints, the Iowa Supreme Court struck down the one in question because of identifiable (and correctable) deficiencies in operation, namely, that the roadblock locations, times, and procedures employed were not established "pursuant to carefully formulated standards and neutral criteria."[11] Checkpoint programs terminated by state supreme courts in Nebraska and Massachusetts are case studies of what will not be judicially tolerated. Under the conditions prevailing in Nebraska, the "driver's reasonable expectation of privacy was rendered subject to arbitrary invasion" and, as such, "Crom was unreasonably seized in violation of the Fourth Amendment."[12] In Massachusetts, motorists were detained late at night, the checkpoint plan had been formulated earlier that day, and the mechanics of its operation—including which vehicles to stop—were left to the discretion of field officers, resulting in a backup of motorists for almost a mile and other hazardous safety conditions.[13]

Third, even when all the conditions in Exhibit 4.1 were met, some courts voided sobriety checkpoints on the grounds that the balancing test tilted toward the motorist's "right to be let alone" because drunk driving roadblocks are ineffective, less-intrusive alternatives are available for accomplishing the state's goal, and the intrusions are not simply "minor inconveniences." Sobriety stops may involve shining flashlights on the driver and inside the car, leaning down to smell driver's breath, and having the driver perform field sobriety tests. As such, the stops necessarily entail a much greater (discretionary) invasion of privacy than would a simple document check.[14]

EFFECTIVENESS OF SOBRIETY CHECKPOINTS

Police administrators themselves agree that checkpoints "are a highly inefficient tactic for catching drunk drivers," as roadblocks are unproductive and a poor allocation of police resources.[15] Overall, only 1 percent of the checkpoint stops result in a DWI arrest. The New Hampshire Supreme Court took the low arrest yield (18/1,680) as confirmation that "roadblocks are not especially effective in snaring drunk drivers. For every 100 vehicles detained for one to five minutes, only one DWI arrest was made. An inordinate number of innocent citizens must be stopped in order to make only a few arrests."[16] The Supreme Court said as much in *Prouse* when it observed that "The contribution to highway safety made by [suspicionless] stops selected from among drivers generally will therefore be marginal at best." Supporters of the practice, however, emphasize that the primary purpose of stopping drivers for a sobriety check is "not to make arrests of drunken drivers but to promote public safety by *deterring* intoxicated persons from driving [in the first place]"; accordingly, the low arrest yield is cited as proof that sobriety checkpoints are highly effective.[17]

Less-Intrusive Alternatives?

Courts in Illinois, Indiana, and New Hampshire have ruled sobriety checkpoints unconstitutional on the grounds that the balancing test justification for airport security and border checks does not apply to drunk driving roadbloacks. This is because there are no less-intrusive alternatives for coping with hijacking and illegal immigration whereas, by contrast, "there are many viable, less intrusive alternatives to the sobriety roadblock" for combating drunk driving, such as highly visible roving patrols or specially trained DWI squads who concentrate their efforts near bars and taverns where accidents regularly occur.[18] Illustrative of the latter option is a group of specially trained Suffolk (N.Y.) highway patrol officers who aggressively search for drunk drivers at night by pulling over suspiciously driven vehicles; the unit made almost half of the

9,000 DWI arrests in 1985. Miami's Selective Enforcement Motor-
cycle Squad consists of thirty-three officers who are specially trained
in spotting drunk drivers and making arrests that hold up in court.
And Omaha has a six-member squad who rely heavily on radar,
because their experience shows that speeding is highly correlated with
drunk driving.[19]

Are Sobriety Checkpoints "Fishing Expeditions?"

The core substantive criticism of sobriety checkpoints is that their
constitutional status should not depend on speculation concerning
their effectiveness, deterrent value, potential for abuse of discretion,
or on the less-intrusive-alternative argument. Rather, drunk driving
roadblocks should be prohibited because "the stops constitute police
seizure and detention in the absence of the faintest scintilla of
criminal wrongdoing. The sole, indeed admitted, purpose for the
stops is *to fish* [emphasis mine] for evidence. Motorists are being held
for no other articulable purpose than satisfaction of investigative
curiosity," and because "they happen to be traveling on a particular
road at a certain time."[20] Courts in Oregon, Oklahoma, and
elsewhere have drawn the ominous implications of the "ends justifies
the means" philosophy behind sobriety checkpoints:[21] if sobriety
checkpoints can be used to screen highways for drunk drivers, "the
next logical step would be to allow similar stops for [ferreting] out
other types of criminal offenders," such as illegal gun owners, drug
traffickers, and car thieves.[22]

Supreme Court Approves Sobriety Checkpoints

Early in 1986, the Michigan Department of State Police established
a pilot sobriety checkpoint program with strict guidelines governing
its operation, site selection, and publicity. In the first implementation
of the program, all 126 vehicles passing through the checkpoint were
detained for about twenty-five seconds each, resulting in the arrest of
two drunk drivers. Applying the balancing test of *Brown*, the State
Court of Appeals ruled that Michigan's checkpoint program violated
the Fourth Amendment because, like sobriety checkpoints in general,
it was ineffective as evidenced by a drunk driving detection (success)
rate of only 1.5 percent [2/126]; hence, in its view such checkpoints
did not manifestly contribute to the state's interest in curbing drunk

Photo 4.1
Stop Ahead—Sobriety Checkpoint Sign

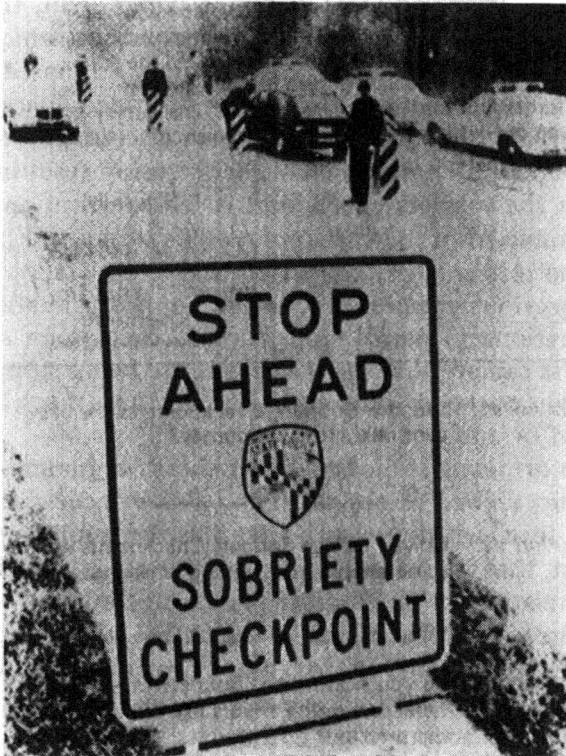

The constitutional status of sobriety checkpoints hinged on whether stopping motorists without individualized reasonable-suspicion violated the Fourth Amendment prohibition against unreasonable seizures. The Supreme Court approved drunk driving roadblocks in 1990 in *Sitz,* by applying a balancing-test analysis to the under-lying issues and likening sobriety checkpoints to the checkpoint stops for detecting illegal aliens whose legal-ity it previously upheld in *Martinez-Fuerte.* Photo cour-tesy of First Sgt. Bill Tower/Maryland State Police.

driving. And while acknowledging that the checkpoints' objective intrusion on individual liberties is slight, the appellate court was of the opinion that their subjective intrusion—in terms of the surprise, fear, and anxiety that the brief detentions generated among stopped drivers—was substantial.

In *Michigan Dept. of State Police* v. *Sitz* (1990), the Supreme Court soundly criticized the two major grounds on which the lower court's invalidation of the checkpoint program was based.[23] Drawing squarely upon its decisions in *Brown* and *Martinez-Fuerte* to analyze the constitutional issue at hand, the Court discounted the subjective intrusion concern by noting that "The intrusion resulting from the brief stop at the sobriety checkpoint is for constitutional purposes indistinguishable from the checkpoint stops we upheld in Martinez-Fuerte." The elements of "surprise" and "fear" about which the Court had previously expressed concern applied primarily to roving (highly discretionary) patrol stops, not to checkpoint stops where "the motorist can see that other vehicles are being stopped, he can see visible signs of the officers' authority, and he is much less likely to be frightened or annoyed by the intrusion."

The Court disposed of the "ineffectiveness" argument—which the Appeals Court viewed as not satisfying *Brown's* dictum concerning "the degree to which the seizure advances the public interest"—by pointing out that in Martinez-Fuerte the ratio of illegal aliens detected in relation to the number of vehicles stopped was just 0.5 percent. Moreover, "the degree to which the seizure advances the public interest" and deciding from among various alternatives which technique should be employed to detect drunk drivers are matters to be left up to the accountable authorities rather than the courts. Accordingly, "the balance of the State's interest in preventing drunken driving, the extent to which this system can reasonably be said to advance that interest, and the degree of intrusion upon individual motorists who are briefly stopped, weighs in favor of the state program. We therefore hold that it is consistent with the Fourth Amendment."

5

Preliminary Breath Tests

Preliminary Breath Testing (PBT) devices are portable, hand-held units that measure the BAC level from a breath sample, taken at roadside, by having the driver blow into a disposable mouthpiece.[1] Because Preliminary (or Pre-arrest) Breath Test results are an objective, chemical indicator of blood alcohol content, they are considered more reliable than the officer's subjective evaluation of intoxication based on the driver's general demeanor and field sobriety tests.[2]

USE OF PRELIMINARY BREATH TESTS

As a roadside screening aid, PBTs are primarily used to establish or verify whether there is probable cause to arrest and, especially in marginal cases, for detecting borderline drunk drivers who might otherwise be able to conceal overt signs of intoxication.[3] Even when PBT information does not justify an arrest, it can be invaluable to the officer in deciding whether the motorist or passengers are sober enough to have the car released to them on the spot.[4] In Washington where 196 PBTs are being used by state troopers working the night shift, 59 percent of the suspects who took the PBT in 1988 were arrested and 69 percent of their passengers who consented to a PBT were not allowed to drive.[5] A report released in November 1988 documented that "two interventions substantially reduce alcohol-related fatalities: the use of preliminary breath tests and sobriety checkpoints. These two interventions were estimated to have decreased fatalities by 7 percent and 12 percent, respectively; the interaction of these interventions together were estimated to have decreased single-vehicle nighttime occupant fatalities by 35 percent.'' Preliminary breath test laws alone might have saved 394 lives per year, and in combination with sobriety checkpoints 3,455 lives might have been saved each year in the United States between 1982 and 1986.[6] As of 1988, thirty-four states provided for preliminary breath testing, a procedure endorsed by the President's Commission on Drunk Driving. Contrary to the commission's recommendation, though, PBT results are usually not admissible at trial for conviction purposes.

PASSIVE ALCOHOL SENSORS

A specialized, *covert* type of PBT is the Passive Alcohol Sensor (PAS; see Photo 5.1), which resembles and ordinary police flashlight but is equipped with a fuel cell sensor. When held within six inches of the driver's mouth, the PAS will detect any alcohol vapor in the air and displays a digital BAC readout on a tiny screen in the flashlight's handle. From start to finish, the entire process takes less than thirty seconds, thereby minimizing any delays or inconvenience to sober drivers who constitute the bulk of drivers stopped at sobriety checkpoints. The PAS is ideally suited for surreptitious use at night when police officers have occasion to shine their flashlight inside the car window to "help" motorists locate their licenses, or as part of the rountine questioning and observation of stopped motorists. Unlike regular overt PBTs, the *passive* alcohol sensor does not require the driver's cooperation in order to obtain a breath sample.[7]

A limitation of the sensor flashlight is that it was designed to detect other hydrocarbons besides alcohol, which are reflected in the PAS readout.[8] It is therefore inadvisable for officers to use PAS results as the sole grounds for making an arrest. Instead, a positive sensor BAC reading should be a signal that further examination of the suspect is called for, by conducting field sobriety tests, gaze nystagmus or an overt PBT.[9]

PAS Project in Charlottesville, Virginia

A well-publicized sobriety checkpoint program was conducted at night during October and November 1984 by the Charlottesville police department. The police used their sensor flashlights on half of the cars stopped to obtain a breath sample (unbeknownst to the drivers), and followed normal checkpoint procedures half the time. Drivers who registered ≥ .05 on the PAS were directed to a secondary area for field sobriety tests and, depending on their performance, were asked to undergo a PBT. If the PBT was .05-.09, the officer gave motorists a written warning for driving while impaired and made them find some other means of transportation home; if the PBT was .10, the driver was arrested. The results of the experiment demonstrated that, by using PAS's in this way, the police were able to increase the detection rate of DWI and alcohol-impaired (.05-.09) motorists by 50 percent and 100 percent, respectively, and make twice as many drunken driving arrests. Moreover, the sensor flashlights reduced the unnecessary detention (from 18 percent to 8 percent) of drivers who consumed no or only small amounts of alcohol, which is especially important since most motorists stopped at sobriety checkpoints are not alcohol impaired.[10]

Legal Objections to PAS's

Some Virginia defense lawyers are adamantly opposed to the use of PAS's on strictly legal grounds. "Virginia law says you don't have to give a breath test until you've been arrested. Now they're doing essentially a breath test as the first step—without probable cause or reasonable suspicion." Counsel for the Traffic Institute at North-Western University believes that PAS's will not be viewed as unreasonable searches by the courts, based on a precedent set in a case involving a narcotics-sniffing dog. "In that case, the Supreme Court held that things open to view and to smell do not involve a search, and that you did not have to have probable cause to do it"—an argument that the critics of PAS's sharply reject: "I seriously question whether the Supreme Court would conclude that the dogs were not doing a search if when you rolled down the car window, the police threw the dogs inside your car, which is exactly what they're doing here [in the Charlottesville roadblock.]"[11]

The use of flashlight sensors as well as overt PBTs may be prohibited under the implied-consent statutes of some states. This is because the requirement that drivers submit to a breath, blood, or urine tests or risk losing their license may not include passive breath tests, or because implied-consent statutes become applicable only upon arrest. Like above-board PBTs, Passive Alcohol Sensor results are not accurate enough to be admitted as evidence at trial on a DWI charge.[12]

Photo 5.1
Collage of Three Photos Illustrating Passive Alcohol Sensor

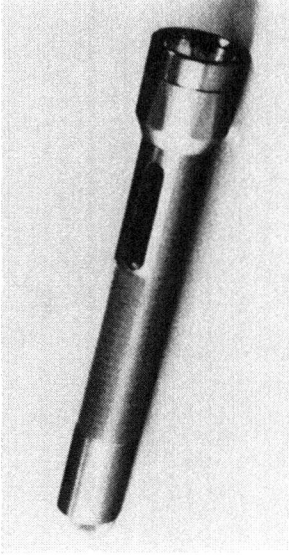

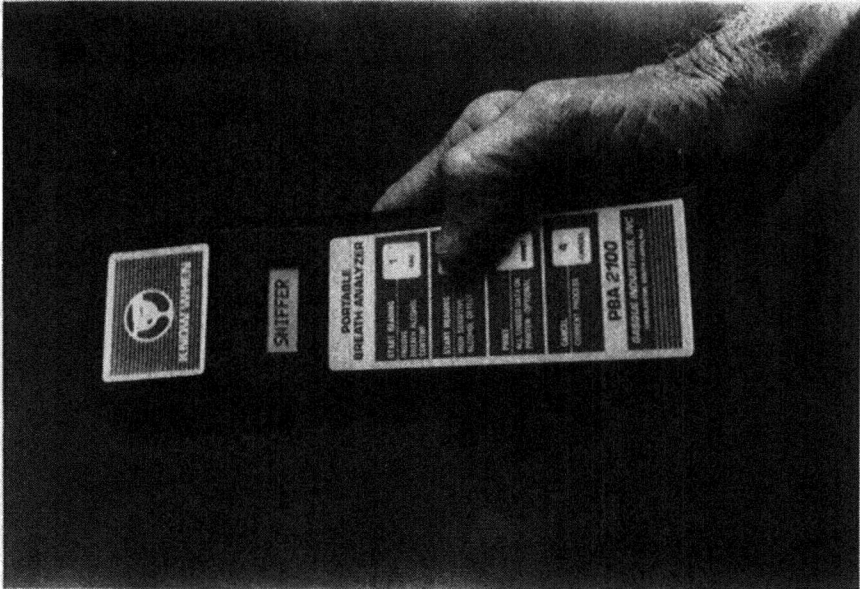

Photo 5.1 A and B. The "Sniffer" is a small, hand-held breath analyzer that measures the ethyl alcohol in the air in any area it is pointed, indicates the BAL, and gives a pass/fail rating. It is being used by the South Carolina Highway Patrol and Myrtle Beach Police Department to supplement standard field sobriety tests. The sniffer was developed by electronic engineer Sam Gasque after his brother narrowly escaped serious injury in a head-on collision with a drunk driver. Photo of "Sniffer" courtesy of Sam Gasque/Know When.

Photo 5.1 C. This Passive Alcohol Sensor that looks like an over-sized flashlight is actually a state-of-the-art breath analyzer. A gauge on the side displays the alcohol content when held within 6 inches of the driver's mouth. Developed under the sponsorship of the Insurance Institute for Highway Safety, the PAS is being used by police in Charlottesville (Virginia) and by officers in Binghamton (N.Y.) who work exclusively on the DWI patrol.

6

Administrative License Suspension

OVERVIEW OF PER SE LAWS

It is common for suspected drunk drivers, upon arrest, to refuse to take a chemical test for intoxication (usually a breathalyzer test) or for their BAC to be .10 or more. Yet, under what used to be ordinary circumstances, the suspects were able to retain their licenses and continue to drive until their licenses were revoked as part of the sentence imposed after conviction, a process that could take months or even a year or more. In order to correct this situation and remove drunk drivers from the road as soon as possible, by July 1990 some twenty-four states (starting with Minnesota in 1976) had enacted administrative per se license suspension laws: drivers arrested for an alcohol-related driving violation who refuse to take a breathalyzer (or other chemical) test or who fail the test can have their licenses suspended in short order.[1] Wisconsin's 1982 administrative license suspension law was the result of lobbying efforts by Mark and Bonnie Schuett, whose four-year-old daughter was killed by a drunk driver as she was walking near her home in Ixonia, Wis. The suspect pleaded no-contest to DWI, was fined $284, and received a five-day suspended jail sentence.[2]

These laws are referred to as "administrative" because the license sanction does not depend upon a judicial finding or trial but is imposed by an administrative agency, ordinarily the state department of motor vehicles; and they are "per se" laws because refusing or failing the chemical test automatically triggers the law's application.[3] These administrative license sanctions are separate from and in addition to any criminal penalties that may be imposed as a result of a DUI prosecution and conviction. It is not at all unusual for drivers who refuse or fail the breathalyzer test (hereafter, "per se violators") whose licenses are suspended to be acquitted in criminal court of the DUI charge, or not even be charged with the offense.[4] The objective of the per se license sanctions is specific deterrence: to deter those whose licenses are suspended for recidivating by guaranteeing swift and certain punishment (the suspension) right after the violation.

Implementation of Per Se Laws

The per se laws are typically implemented in the following manner. The arresting officer takes the per se violator's driver's license on the spot, gives the subject a receipt for the confiscated license, and forwards the license to the state's licensing agency for suspension action. The subject's receipt serves as a temporary driver's license (good for 30 to 45 days) pending the outcome of the administrative hearing.[5] If the motorist does not request a hearing to challenge the impending revocation within the time specified by law, the suspension automatically goes into effect; otherwise, the suspension becomes final if and when the licensing agency rules against the driver. The revocation period is usually longer for those who refuse (180 days) to take the test than for those who fail it (60 to 90 days); and repeaters receive longer suspensions than do first offenders; in Illinois, for instance, the former receive a twelve-month suspension compared to three months for the latter.[6] The per se statutes intentionally put the affected drivers "between a rock and a hard place" because they must choose between two unfavorable alternatives: if they refuse or fail a breathalyzer test their license is forfeited; if they take and fail the test, the incriminating test results can be used at trial against them.[7]

PRACTICES THAT UNDERMINE PER SE LAWS

Immediate Prehearing Suspension

The temporary license granted suspended drunk drivers while awaiting the outcome of the hearing patently weakens the potential

Photo 6.1
License Suspension Poster: "If You Drink and Drive"

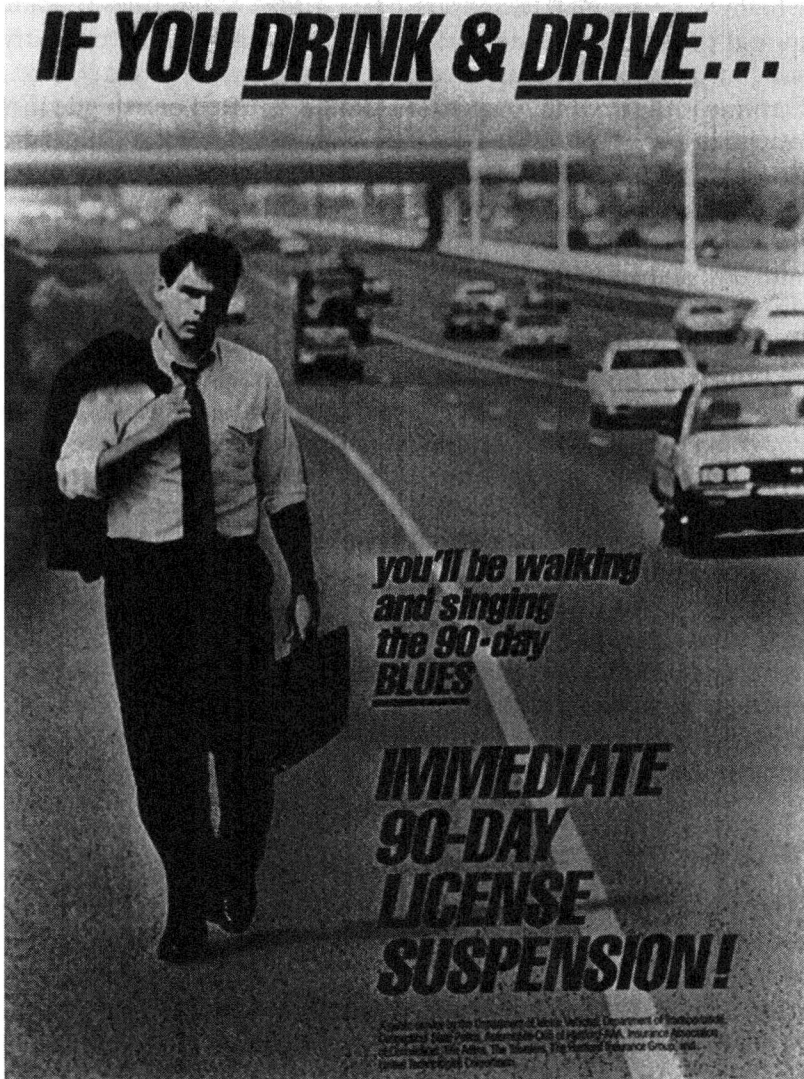

Administrative license suspension. In many states drivers who, upon arrest, refuse to take or fail a breathalyzer test are subject to administrative license suspension sanctions, which operate independently of any criminal action taken against the suspect or the outcome of prosecution. These laws are geared toward "specific deterrence" by implementing swift and certain punishment. The Surgeon General's Panel of Experts as well as the AAA Foundation for Traffic Safety recommended a "hard" license suspension without the possibility of obtaining an occupational or hardship exemption.

benefits of per se laws. To keep per se offenders from returning to the highways even on a temporary basis, a 1986 Massachusetts statute required the licencing authority to impose an immediate prehearing license suspension pending a regular hearing within twenty days to determine if the original suspension should be lifted or extended.[8] An arrested driver who refused to take a breathalyzer test and whose license was immediately suspended without a hearing claimed that his constitutional right to due process was violated.

In *Mackey* v. *Montrym* (1979), the Supreme Court upheld the summary prehearing suspension policy in Massachusetts on the grounds that the need to remove immediately a drunk driver from the road was an "emergency" that it likened to immediately removing contaminated food or mislabeled drugs from the marketplace.[9] Applying the balancing test, the Court made it clear that the compelling "state interest"—in deterrence, highway safety, and obtaining relevant evidence for subsequent criminal proceedings— justified the summary prehearing action, when the latter is followed by due process protections in the form of a hearing.

Responding in a slightly different way to the same problem addressed by the Massachusetts statute, in 1982 Minnesota made the temporary license good for only seven days, after which the license is revoked; and even if a hearing is requested the license remains suspended until the outcome of the hearing.[10] In New York, repeaters have their licenses suspended immediately, pending disposition on the criminal charges of DWI.[11]

Need for "Hard" Suspension

The weakest link in the per se laws is that exemptions may be granted by the licensing authority if the suspension would create an undue "occupational hardship" (e.g., their livelihood depends on driving), or if it would prevent attending treatment programs and they have no other means of transportation available.[12] "The Maryland Legislature has made a serious mistake by permitting work-related exceptions to the law. To be an effective deterrent, license sanctions must be swift and certain. This loophole compromises both swiftness and certainty."[13] A substantial number (about 30 percent) of suspects refuse to take a breathalyzer test, request a hearing, and clog the system with endless appeals in the hope of obtaining a work-related hardship license allowing them to drive under restricted circumstances. Ironically, the problem that work-related exceptions seeks to address and prevent rarely occurs. A 1986 study in Delaware found that just 1.5 percent of the offenders lost their jobs or were unable to receive treatment because of the suspension. And, invariably, those who did suffer had positions that required them to drive on the job, such as school bus drivers—who should have lost their jobs in view of the circumstances leading up to their license suspension.[14] To rectify this situation, almost every reform group has recommended adopting a "hard" driver's license revocation policy: no exceptions would be made for personal hardship, occupational necessity, to attend alcohol abuse treatment programs, or for any other reason.[15] The President's Commission On Drunk Driving recommended that occupational exemptions should only be granted on a very limited basis and "in no event should this be done for repeat offenders."[16]

Suspensions Ignored

Nationwide, as many as 70 to 80 percent of the drivers whose licenses are suspended simply continue to drive without them or easily obtain a new license in other states; in 1977, for example, Ohio issued 1.3 million more licenses than the number of driving-age state residents.[17] Clarence Busch, the California drunk driver who killed Cari Lightner in 1980, moved to Wisconsin in 1981, where he easily obtained another driver's license within a few days.[18] Busch's application might have been denied by Wisconsin authorities had an effective National Driver Register system been in place at that time (see Close-up 6.1). The surgeon general's panel of experts recommended that persons found driving on a suspended license should have their license plates confiscated or their vehicles impounded.[19]

Close-up 6.1: The National Driver Register

The National Driver Register (NDR), established by Congress in 1960, was a central repository of information on license suspensions, application denials and the like, that was intended to assist states in identifying and taking appropriate action against out-of-state "bad apple" drivers. Under the original NDR system, requested information had to be mailed out and, with 84,000 inquiries a day, the states were unable to obtain the requested data in an efficient and timely manner.[a] Congress corrected this flaw in 1982 by establishing a computerized National Driver Register, containing the names of people convicted of serious traffic violations and license sanctions, that could provide the requested information instantaneously. Of the 545,000 inquiries submitted in four tests sites, it resulted in identifying (within seven seconds per request) and denying licenses to some 20,830 problem drivers—84 percent of whom were denied while the applicant was waiting for license approval "at the counter."[b]

[a]*Newsweek,* September 13, 1982, p. 39.
[b]*Network Newsnotes,* Fall 1989, p. 4.

PER SE LAWS TOP PRIORITY AND HIGHLY EFFECTIVE

Administrative license suspension has been unanimously endorsed by reform groups as their number-one priority and is a key provision in the Drunk Driving Prevention Act of 1988 (see Exhibit 6.1). "For years the National Commission Against Drunk Driving has maintained that administrative license sanctions may be the single most effective means of reducing drunk driving crashes in the short term."[20] The strength of per se laws is that they operate as a specific deterrent by quickly taking identified offenders off the road and

Exhibit 6.1
Drunk Driving Prevention Act of 1988

Passed as part of the federal government's Omnibus Drug Bill, this act made $125 million available to states, to be used for a variety of programs to curb drunken driving. To be eligible for these incentive grants, the states must first implement the following six drunk driving countermeasures. Sen. Frank Lautenberg, who authored the legislation, considered administrative revocation laws a key provision of the Act.

- administrative license sanctions (at least three months for first offenders, one year for repeat offenders.)
- self-funding enforcement programs.
- .10 BAC per se level.
- mandatory blood alcohol testing of drivers in fatal or serious crashes.
- distinctive driver licenses for drivers under age of 21.
- passage of open container laws.

Source: Drunk Driving Prevention Act of 1988, Title VIII of Drug Bill; Sen. Frank Lautenberg, "Perspective," *Network Newsnotes,* Summer 1989, p. 3.

Photo 6.2
Senator Frank Lautenberg

Senator Frank Lautenberg, chief sponsor of the act, emphasized administrative revocation laws as its key provision. "Administrative revocation works because it ensures that punishment is both sure and swift." The act also encourages states to confiscate the license plates of motorists who continue to drive with suspended licenses.

reducing recidivism among this group.[21] All of the studies indicate that license suspension appears to be a more promising deterrent to drunk driving than any other single countermeasure, including treatment or a mandatory jail term (discussed later).[22]

Effectiveness of Per Se Laws

A study released in March 1988 by the Insurance Institute for Highway Safety found that administrative revocation laws were the single most effective tool in battling drunk drivers, cutting nighttime traffic fatalities by 9 percent.[23] Separate studies conducted in four states revealed that in each state the license suspensions were more effective than treatment in preventing further accidents among repeat offenders.[24] The researchers noted that in California, "persons who were suspended for test refusal were found to have 72.2 percent fewer crashes during the six month suspension period than persons who licenses were not suspended, and during the initial 18 months following the term of the suspension they continued to register 57.8 percent fewer crashes than the group that was not suspended."[25] And a study by Sigmastat found that "some form of license sanction holds the promise for deterring drunk driving, with 35 percent of the licensing-sanction states exhibiting statistically significant reductions in driver fatal crash alcohol involvement during the period of implementation."[26] In 1986, Minnesota revoked the licenses of

42,586 drunk drivers for at least three months, including 8,468 for refusing and 28,080 for failing the test. The state's stringent suspension policy is given a large share of the credit for the sharp reduction in alcohol-related crashes, "and an all-time record low traffic death rate in Minnesota of 1.6 per 100 million vehicle miles" in 1987.[27] And even though many people continue to drive after their licenses have been revoked, studies show that they drive fewer miles and more carefully than they did before the suspension.[28]

7

Prosecuting Drunk Drivers

Prosecutors and courts around the country are responding to drunk driving with new evidentiary aids, tactics, and rulings that are reshaping the way that DUI cases are being prosecuted and defended.

MIRANDA WARNINGS AT ROADSIDE QUESTIONING

Miranda Warnings Not Required

In January 1985 a police office in Newtown Township (Pa.) stopped Thomas Bruder for erratic driving and ignoring a red light. Smelling alcohol and observing Bruder's stumbling movements, the officer administered field sobriety tests (which Bruder failed) and also inquired about alcohol consumption, to which Bruder replied that he had been drinking. Bruder was then arrested and given the Miranda warnings. The issue before the Supreme Court in *Bruder* (1988), and in a remarkably similar case, *Berkemer* (1984), was the following: should the incriminating statements made at roadside *before* the suspect was Mirandized have been admitted into evidence at trial for DUI?[1]

Miranda warnings are triggered by custodial interrogation, which occurs after arrest and usually takes place at a police station, and are intended to prevent the police from eliciting involuntary or coerced confessions from suspects being interviewed in police-dominated physical surroundings, "on police turf." In both *Bruder* and *Berkemer,* the Supreme Court stressed that the subjects were not under arrest when the damaging statements were made, and the absence of coercive elements associated with bona fide custodial interrogation at a police station. Traffic stops commonly occur in the "public view," in an atmosphere "far less police dominated than that surrounding the kinds of interrogation at issue in *Miranda,*" and "the detainee is not obliged to respond" to the officer's roadside questions. Accordingly, the Court almost summarily disposed of the Bruder case by citing its ruling in *Berkemer:* "the noncoercive aspects of ordinary traffic stops prompts us to hold that persons temporarily detained pursuant to such stops are not 'in custody' for the purposes of Miranda [warnings]." Motorists stopped for cause or at sobriety checkpoints are therefore not entitled to be given the Miranda warnings because they are not technically in police custody and because their responses to police questions are presumptively uncoerced.

ADMISSIBILITY OF REFUSAL EVIDENCE

> If a person refuses to submit to chemical analysis of his blood, urine, breath or other bodily substance and that person subsequently stands trial for driving while under the influence of alcohol or drugs . . . such refusal may be admissible into evidence at trial.
> —South Dakota Laws Annotated, 1980

Refusal Evidence Admissible at Trial

In July 1980, Mason Neville was stopped by two Madison (S.Dak.) police officers for ignoring a stop sign. Neville staggered out of the car smelling of alcohol and told them his driver's license had been revoked in connection with a previous DWI conviction. After failing two field sobriety tests, Neville was arrested, Mirandized, agreed to talk without a lawyer, and was taken to a police station. For a third time they asked Neville to take a bood alcohol test and warned him that he could lose his driver's license for not complying, but Neville again refused to take the test: "I'm too drunk. I won't pass the test."[2]

At the state court level Neville successfully contended that allowing his refusal to be introduced as evidence against him at trial would violate his Fifth Amendment protection against self-incrimination. In *Neville,* however, the Supreme Court held that "a refusal to take a blood-alcohol test, after a police officer has lawfully requested it, is not an act coerced by the officer, and thus is not protected by the privilege against self-incrimination." Since Neville had a choice of whether or not to refuse the blood alcohol test, his refusal was a voluntary act—he was not "compelled to be a witness against himself"—even though a refusal might entail administrative penalties.[3] The Fifth Amendment does not prevent police from asking arrested Mirandized suspects to take a chemical sobriety test, the prosecutor from using that evidence at trial, or—pursuant to the implied-consent laws found in every state—the police from *forcing* suspects to submit to a blood alcohol test (see Close-up 7.1).

The Illinois Revised Statutes (1983) is an example of "implied-consent" laws. It states:

Any person who drives or is in actual physical control of a motor vehicle upon the public highways of this state shall be deemed to have given his consent to a chemical test or tests of blood, breath, or urine for the purposes of determining the alcohol, other drug, or combination thereof content of such person's blood if the person is arrested for driving a motor vehicle while under the influence of intoxicants in violation of [state statute] or a municipal ordinance. A test shall be administered upon the request of a police officer having reasonable grounds to believe the person arrested to have been driving while under the influence of intoxicants in violation of [state statute] or of a municipal ordinance.

The *Neville* decision was a boon to prosecuting drunk drivers because it eliminated one of the most common obstacles to securing convictions. Regardless of how the refusal is conveyed,[4] refusal-evidence may now be presented to the jury, who can draw whatever inferences they choose. The state's interest in presenting refusal-evidence, as its main case or in closing argument, is twofold: to explain why the actual chemical test results are unavailable; and the refusal will almost invariably be considered indicative of the defendant's own consciousness of guilt.[5] And should defendants feel obliged to take the stand to explain their reasons for refusing, the prosecutor may seek to impeach their credibility by introducing evidence of their prior driving record.[6]

Close-up 7.1: Self Incrimination and Physical Evidence

While drunk driving suspects may refuse to submit to a chemical sobriety test, the police do not have to take "no" for an answer: they can use reasonable force to obtain a blood sample without the driver's consent.

In the seminal case, Schmerber was hospitalized after a car accident in which he was the driver. Observing signs of intoxication at both the accident scene and the hospital, a police officer placed Schmerber under arrest and gave him the Miranda warnings. On the advice of counsel, Schmerber refused to consent to the blood test. But at the instruction of the police officer, the attending physician forcibly extracted a blood sample, whose results were used to convict Schmerber of DUI at trial.

The Supreme Court rejected the claim that the forcible administration of the blood alcohol test was a violation of his self-incrimination privilege. "We hold that the privilege [against self-incrimination] protects an accused only from being compelled to testify against himself, or otherwise provide the State with evidence of a *testimonial* or *communicative* nature [italics mine] . . . Compulsion which makes the suspect or accused the source of 'real or physical evidence' does not violate" the Fifth Amendment.[a] Because the self-incrimination safeguard does not apply to nontestimonial (physical) evidence, under certain conditions the police may employ force in the process of utilizing the human body as a source of physical (nontestimonial) evidence. In 1989, the Ninth U.S. Circuit Court ruled that it was not an "unreasonable search and seizure" when police handcuffed a protesting drunk driving suspect to a chair and pinned him to the floor so that a lab technician could withdraw blood.[b] "The 'force' used by Officer Zatarian in this case was nothing more than the application of physical restraint required to conduct the blood extraction in a safe and efficient manner."[c]

There are, of course, limits to how far the police may go in conducting invasive bodily searches without violating due process. These limits are exceeded if the conduct of the police is considered "shocking to the conscience" or is patently "offense to human dignity," as was the situation in *Rochin* v. *California*.[d] In *Rochin* the Supreme Court reversed the drug possession conviction of a man who underwent a forced stomach-pumping at the direction of the police, in order to retrieve two morphine capsules he swallowed when the police entered his room.

a *Schmerber* v. *California,* 384 U.S. 757 (1966).

b*National Law Journal,* September 18, 1989, p. 6.

c*ABA Journal,* December 1989, p. 80.

d*Rochin* v. *California,* 342 U.S. 165 (1952).

Dilatory Tactics Eschewed

In the case of drunk drivers, their Sixth Amendment right to counsel includes a reasonable opportunity to consult with counsel before deciding whether to submit to a blood alcohol test. Nonetheless, several state courts have held that exercising this right cannot interfere with "the timely and efficacious administration of the test."[7] If counsel cannot be contacted within a reasonable time, the arrested driver must decide whether to comply with the testing request or risk license forfeiture and the *Neville* consequences. The concern behind adopting this position is that drivers would delay taking the test—on the pretext of waiting to contact their attorneys—until their blood alcohol level significantly diminished through normal physiological processes. This same consideration also usually makes it impractical to first request a search warrant authorizing the invasive body search.[8]

PRESERVATION OF BREATH SAMPLES

After California police stopped two drivers and gave them breath tests that they failed (over .10), the police destroyed the breath samples in accordance with their normal practice. The defendants claimed that preservation of the samples would have enabled them to impeach the incriminating test results at trial. Concurring, the California Court of Appeals suppressed the introduction of the unfavorable test results at a DUI trial on the grounds that due process required the arresting officers to preserve the breath samples.

This is no question that the due process clause of the Fourteenth Amendment requires the state to disclose favorable (exculpatory) evidence to the defendant, that is, forbids withholding or destroying evidence that would tend to exonerate the accused. In *Trombetta,* however, the Court held that the due process clause does not require law enforcement agencies to preserve breath samples in order to introduce the results of the chemical analysis at trial.[9] This is because the "breath samples were much more likely to provide inculpatory [unfavorable] than exculpatory evidence," and the defendants had other means available at trial for impeaching the incriminating test results without having to resort to the actual breath samples.

VIDEOTAPING SUSPECTS

Since a picture is worth a thousand words, police videotaping of drunk driving suspects, at roadside or at the police station, can be an invaluable aid to facilitating convictions. By graphically depicting the suspect's behavior, videotaped evidence can enhance the officer's observational testimony in court and can make such an indelible impression on a jury[10] that it often leads defense attorneys to change their clients' pleas to guilty. The Massachusetts police began regularly to videotape drunk driving arrests in 1985.[11] Westport's (Conn.) introduction of videotapes in the early 1980s helped the city achieve a near-perfect record of DWI convictions. In one case, a suspect pretended to faint in the booking room but quickly revived himself when the officer left the room, unaware that a video camera was recording his feigning spell. "Some of them can't even stand up when arrested. That's very graphic evidence."[12]

The Bountiful Police Department (near Salt Lake City, Utah) uses video cameras mounted in their patrol vehicles to record the events leading up to the stop and everything else that transpires at roadside, in addition to videotaping the suspect's postarrest behavior at the police station. This expansive use of videotaping "has become so effective in the courtroom that local defense attorneys are attacking every possible aspect to keep it from being entered as evidence."[13] The mere prospect of videotape being used as evidence at trial is why the Bountiful police had to introduce it in court only once in two years.

The suspect's performance of sobriety tests, regardless of where they are administered, can be especially damaging in court. According to the American Bar Association, "videotaping of physical sobriety tests raises no self incrimination issues—even though the test results are often highly inculpatory—because the performance of those tests is 'demonstrative' [physical], not 'testimonial' evidence."[14] Not all courts share this viewpoint, however. The Iowa Court of Appeals ruled that the police cannot

Photo 7.1
Bountiful Police Department Video-Equipped Cars

The Bountiful Police Department (Utah) videotapes the events leading up to their stopping suspected drunk drivers as well as the field sobriety tests. Although the Supreme Court has yet to rule specifically on this issue, such videotaped evidence probably does not violate the suspect's self-incrimination protection because the videotaped behavior is "nontestimonial" evidence. Photo courtesy of Bountiful Police Department/Det. Lloyd Kilpack.

make videotapes of arrested drunk driving suspects who refuse to take physical sobriety tests, because a videotape "can only be interpreted as an attempt to have the defendant condemn himself by communicating by his actions his refusal to take the tests."[15]

ILLEGAL PER SE LAWS

DUI a Per Se Offense

Illegal per se laws provide that if the accused was driving with a BAC that exceeded the legal limit, the defendant will be convicted of DWI on the basis of that material fact alone, thereby making chemical test results (the "evidential" BAC) the state's most probative evidence.[16] Under illegal per se statutes, it is unnecessary for the prosecutor to prove anything else to prevail in court. With 46 states having adopted .10 illegal per se laws by 1989, it is now the norm that DWI defendants are presumed to be intoxicated at .10—a presumption that cannot be refuted by defense counsel.[17] Since Pennsylvania passed a per se law making drivers with a .10 BAC automatically guilty of drunken driving, over 25,000 people have been convicted of DWI in that state.[18]

Breathalyzer Tests

The most common method for obtaining evidential chemical test results is by measuring breath samples with a breathalyzer, the generic term for various types of breath testing devices that gained widespread attention starting in 1954 when the first one was introduced.[19] The breathalyzer machine, introduced by Smith & Wesson in 1968, has since been used in nearly 10,000 police departments.[20] The breathalyzer is the standard device used by police for measuring BAC because it is less intrusive, faster, and less embarrassing than collecting urine or blood samples.[21] To be admissible as evidential BAC, breathalyzer equipment must be checked for accuracy and operated according to guidelines specified in the per se legislation, by the courts or by other state authorities.[22] The Massachusetts per se law, for example, requires that breathalyzer equipment be validated four times a year. In California, the Intoxilyzer must be properly prepared before using it, two samples are taken from the suspect that must be within 0.02 of each other to be admissible in court, and the machine is calibrated for accuracy on a weekly basis.[23]

The chemical tests used to determine the evidential BAC can only be given after arrest at a police station (the usual place) or at any other facility having trained operators and the proper testing equipment available.[24] Evidential testing might even take place in "BATmobiles," mobile vans located at sobriety checkpoint sites. In the Charlottesville experiment, drivers who registered .10 on the Passive Alcohol Sensor (a nonevidential BAC) were arrested on the spot and asked to submit to an evidential breath test in the BATmobile.[25] Los Angeles has also used mobile testing, booking, and holding-cell trailers as part of its crackdown on drunk drivers.[26]

Advantages of Per Se Laws

Fewer legal resources are needed to prosecute successfully drunk driving cases because the per se laws reduce the number of legal issues that can arise at trial. As a result, defendants are more likely to plead quilty to DWI rather than contest the charge, and they are less likely to hold out for a plea bargain because the accused has little to bargain with.[27] (In 1978 when no per se law was in effect, California allowed 80,000 drivers arrested for DUI to plead guilty to reckless driving.)[28] It is much more difficult for defense attorneys to cast doubt on scientific breathalyzer results than to discredit an officer's observational and judgmental testimony.[29] Whereas in the past, the breathalyzer was looked upon as little more than a mechanical confirmation of what police officers could determine on their own, under illegal per se, "anybody who flunks a breath test is [guilty of driving] under the influence of alcohol."[30] Judges in Hennepin County (Minnesota) are now relying on breathalyzer test results as the primary evidence in almost all drunk driving cases.[31]

The one notable disadvantage to illegal per se offense laws is that they may be increasing the number of suspects who are refusing to take an evidentiary BAC test, realizing that doing so will probably seal their fate at trial.[32] Their decision not to consent to the test is a very rational one since defendants may be able to explain to the jury's satisfaction why they refused, or the refusal-evidence might be given minimal weight by the factfinder regardless of whether the accused takes the stand.

8

Defending Drunk Drivers

New laws making it more difficult to avoid conviction, hardening public attitudes toward the offense, and stiffer penalties (including mandatory jail) have altered the course and nature of legal representation in drunken driver cases. The same factors exposing drunken drivers to greater jeopardy are responsible for a growing cadre of lawyers and law firms earning a reputation and lucrative income by specializing in their defense (see Close-up 8.1). Whereas before 1980 there were only a handful of lawyers regularly involved in trying drunk driving cases, there are now well over 100 throughout the country who are capitalizing on this new market. The get-tough approach toward middle-class offenders who can afford hefty legal fees has made defending drunk drivers—once considered "the garbage of the law business"—a lucrative new subdivision of the legal profession. In New Jersey, for example, Francis Moore's five-member firm handles 1,000-1,500 drunk driving cases a year, on retainers that run as high as $5,000.[1]

Increasingly, lawyers are pursuing every legal avenue and technicality to have cases dismissed before trial, or devising ingenious strategies for winning acquittals in court. For example, in Broward County (Florida), a jury acquitted Sandra Rosenthal of drunken driving because her lawyer convinced them her accident was caused by an allergic reaction to a combination of chocolate mousse and a drink she had during happy hour; the jury was unaware that Rosenthal had a previous conviction for drunken driving.[2]

CHALLENGING BREATHALYZER TESTS

Because of illegal per se laws, defense attorneys can no longer try to show that even though the accused had a .10 BAC, he or she was not "impaired" or "under the influence." And there is no point in seeking to discredit the breathalyzer machine itself, since "courts throughout the country have recognized its reliability for at least 35 years."[3] Instead, the principal line of defense has shifted[4] to challenging the accuracy of breathalyzer test results because of some impropriety in how the equipment was maintained or prepared for use, or in how the test was administered.[5] Faulty chemical testing machines account for most of the cases won by defense counsel in trial court, and thousands of DWI convictions have been questioned because of improperly calibrated machines or other flaws resulting in false breathalyzer readings.[6]

A pending Chicago lawsuit seeks to invalidate all drunk driving arrests (50,000), convictions, and license suspensions based on breathalyzer tests taken between 1976 and 1988 in the state. During that time, the Illinois State Police were allowed to mix the chemical solution used to calibrate the Intoxilyzer in their own homes, without any independent verification of the machine's accuracy.[7]

In New York City, 80 percent of the drunken driving prosecutions were put on hold, and hundreds of convictions are expected to be reopened due to suspect breathalyzer tests. The chemical solutions supplied by Systems Innovation Inc. and used by police throughout New York State from 1986 to 1989 may have been prepared under substandard manufacturing procedures, thereby compromising the reliability of the tests. The possibility of tainted evidence came to light in the DWI trial of Carlton Coach, who was acquitted. A defense witness who formerly worked for Systems Innovation testified that a key chemical element used in the breathalyzer had been produced in a "slipshod" manner and covered up by the company with fake invoice numbers.[8] According to Don Bailey, the former Pennsylvania auditor general who investigated Systems Innovation, "They definitely were putting out an inferior product."[9]

Chemical vapors inhaled on the job from such products as paint, floor finish, and cement may contaminate the breathalyzer reading and be used to create a reasonable doubt in the jury's mind. Even though Scott Warren had a .10 BAC on the Intoxilyzer, he was acquitted of DWI because defense counsel established that the device construed paint fumes as alcohol. Similarly, a Georgia lawyer got DWI charges dismissed because his client had been putting a finish on a gymnasium floor shortly before being tested for drunk driving.[10]

EXTRAPOLATION ARGUMENT

Depending upon a number of physiological variables, a breathalyzer test taken within a short time after the motorist is stopped could give an inflated estimate of the BAC at the time the person was actually driving. Ideally, the time delay between driving and testing "should be set low enough[11] to provide a reasonable assurance that, despite the test delay, an individual's BAC was above a given limit at the time he or she was driving."[12] Most illegal per se laws, however, make no provision for taking this factor into consideration and simply define DUI in terms of the chemical test result whenever it was administered; a few statutes specify that the test must be given within two hours of the driving behavior to support a per se conviction.[13]

Lawyers intent on utilizing this "last-gulp" defense are fighting an uphill battle. About an hour after John Tischio was stopped for erratic driving, he was given two breathalyzer tests at police headquarters, registered .11, and was convicted under the state's per se law. In a six to one decision, the New Jersey Supreme Court rejected defense counsel's argument that the police should have "extrapolated backwards" to establish the BAC level at the time Tischio was driving: "We rule that it is the blood-alcohol level at the time of the Breathalyzer test that constitutes the essential evidence of the offense." The ruling also, in effect, bars defense counsel from introducing expert witnesses to challenge breathalyzer tests that are administered within a "reasonable time" after being stopped, which was previously one of the most common grounds for getting convictions reversed.[14]

LEGAL WORKSHOPS ON DRUNKEN DRIVER DEFENSES

School for Scoundrels?

In their zeal to leave no stone unturned in representing their clients, lawyers are sponsoring and attending legal workshops and conferences on defending drunken drivers, at which the "tricks of the trade" for getting clients off are examined, shared, and refined. Don Nichols, distinguished editor of the *Drinking/Driving Law Letter,* and Reese Joye, for example, run a legal workshop on drunk driving defenses, under the trade name Continuing Education Seminars, which goes on fifteen-city tours, drawing as many as 100 local attorneys at the one-day sessions, which cost $160 per participant.[15]

Many lawyers participate in these forums and adopt an "anything goes" attitude as a reaction to illegal per se laws that, they believe, deprive defendants of the presumption of innocence. "Unfortunately, when you're arrested for drunk driving, you're already presumed guilty."[16] The workshop agenda for "beating the rap" typically contains the following recommendations:

• Shift the focus of the trial away from BAC readings to casting doubt on the testing machine's reliability. "Constantly attack that machine. Never refer to it as an instrument—that has a scientific aura. Jurors understand machines; their own washing machines break down."

• Minimize the significance of field sobriety tests. Question the conditions under which the field tests were administered.

• Attack the officer's observations and judgment. Don't all cars "weave" on the highway? "Slurred" speech compared to what?[17]

• If they have a choice, drivers should "take a urine test; it is notoriously unreliable. Otherwise, take the breath test. Whatever you do, don't take the blood test. It's too accurate."[18]

• Try to trip up the arresting officer on details about the scene of the arrest. "If they [make mistakes], I can argue, 'Well, if you can't remember this, why can you remember anything else better?'"

• Opt for a jury trial. "I can manipulate the jury's minds more than I can a trial judge who's been on the bench fifteen years and seen all my tricks."[19]

Any questions, class?

Close-up 8.1: If You're Arrested For Drunken Driving, Who You Gonna Call?*

Why, Richard Essen of course, the nation's preeminent drunken driver defense attorney—if you can afford his standard $2,500-$5,000 fee.

In the late 1960s, Essen's principal clientele consisted of murderers and drug dealers. Having qualms about the morality of defending such unsavory clients, Essen decided to concentrate his efforts in the lower (misdemeanor) courts, which were inundated with drunken driving cases and where he honed his skills defending this group of offenders. That career change and the expertise acquired turned out to be propitious. "I didn't go into this [specialty] as a matter of principle. It was a business decision. This was a great opportunity and I took advantage of it." Of the 3,000 drunken driving cases handled by Essen's firm, only 18 have been lost; and they have yet to lose a case that went to trial. "I consider it a moral defeat if we have to go to trial. The idea is to win on motions. You have to make enough requests to keep the state responding."

*After drinking beer for much of the night, Patrick O'Reilly rammed his car into a truck and killed a passenger. O'Reilly, not seriously hurt, had a .13 BAC and was charged with DUI-manslaughter, which carried a maximum penalty of fifteen years in Florida. Essen got the blood test suppressed as inadmissible evidence because it had been taken by a nurse whose license had expired two months earlier and "the statute says the test has to be taken by a licensed nurse." Without that evidence, the state allowed the defendant to plead guilty in exchange for a "withheld adjudication," under which O'Reilly was given three years probation and could have his sentence expunged after that.

*After leaving a football game, a businessman was arrested for driving the wrong way on a one-way street and registered a .14 on a breath test. With two prior DUI convictions, he stood to lose his license for ten years if convicted again. Essen was able to get the case dismissed because the test results were recorded on the wrong form.

Essen boasts that he has a defense strategy, tactic, and approach to cover every situation. Bloodshot eyes? "Contact lenses, smoking, crying, there are dozens of things other than alcohol that can cause bloodshot eyes." Weaving on the road? "They could be falling asleep. They could be reaching for a lighted cigarette that fell. We've had cases of bees in the window." An incriminating breathalyzer test? "If you have chewing gum in your mouth when you take the breath test, that can cause an inaccurate reading." One of his most reliable methods for winning cases is by delay. Florida has a "speedy trial" law requiring drunken driving cases to be brought within ninety days or be dismissed, which Essen exploits unabashedly by scheduling depositions when prosecution witnesses cannot be there.

Essen may not relish relying on legal technicalities but feels that he no longer has any choice because of the public outcry against drunk driving. "The defense of DUI isn't what it used to be. The jury used to think, 'There but for the grace of God go I.' Now they've been so sensitized to the dangers of driving and drinking that there's been an overreaction." MADD president Candy Lightner and other reformers are understandably incensed by Essen's tactics. "He is trying to undo everything we're working for." Ironically, Essen has received more criticism for defending drunk drivers than "when he got a murderer off because a police officer didn't read somebody their Miranda rights"—a poignant sign of how much progress has been made in the war on drunk drivers?

*Sources: Wall Street Journal, April 14, 1986, 1, 24; People Magazine, September 15, 1986, p. 111-115; "Drunk Drivers Get Off," Sally Jessy Raphael program, Transcript # 228.

9

Mandatory Sentences for Drunk Drivers

STIFFER PENALTIES

The punitive attitude that characterizes the initiative against drunk driving is nowhere more compellingly expressed than by the increased penalties contained in the new and revised DUI laws, laws that allow, encourage, or require judges to hand out stiffer sentences upon conviction. In the past, the state penal codes emphasized releasing convicted drunk drivers with a warning, small fines, occasional license suspensions, probation, and treatment program sentences. Although jail sentences have been on the books for over seventy years and could be imposed at the courts' discretion, they were rarely invoked, even for repeat offenders.[1] Regardless of what dispositions were formally permitted at that time, the application of criminal sanctions was notoriously lax so that drunk drivers had little to fear or lose at the sentencing stage.[2]

By contrast, the distinctive features of the stringent reform DUI statutes includes mandatory jail sentences as the number-one priority, substantial fines (up to $1,500 or more), community service, and a downgrading of treatment programs as the principal or only sanction imposed. In order to remove any obstacles that might interfere with incarcerating drunk drivers, several states[3] have banned or placed restrictions on plea bargaining, charge reductions, and prosecutorial diversion. Controlling or limiting the prosecutor's authority to substitute a lesser, nonalcohol charge removes the opportunity for drunk drivers "to hide in a labyrinth of charges and convictions for offenses that are unrelated to those involving alcohol" and facilitates the identification of DWI recidivists.[4] Before California restricted plea bargaining under its completely revised 1982 DUI law, the state was allowing 80,000 drivers a year to plead guilty to reckless driving.[5]

MANDATORY JAIL SENTENCES

Under the new statutes, the provision for and length of mandatory sentences depends on whether the convicted defendant is a first- or second-time DUI offender (see Table 9.1), the consequences of the offense, and possibly even on the offender's having a BAC well above the legal limit.[6] By 1984, seventeen states had mandatory jail terms of one to three days for first offenders, with two days being the norm—virtually unheard of before society got MADD; and forty-two states had prescribed jail terms of two to ninety days for second offenders, most of which were for one month or less.[7] Although possible, longer terms are rarely forthcoming unless there was an accident involving serious injury, the defendant faces manslaughter or murder charges (see Close-up 9.1), or the drunk driving incident occurred in connection with some other crime.[8] Jimmy Grey, who killed two people less than a mile from the tavern where he spent the evening drinking, was convicted of murder and sentenced to seventy years, certainly one of the longest sentences on record for a drunk driving fatality.[9]

In the process of striving to accommodate every possible sentencing goal, many of the beefed-up DUI statutes incorporating mandatory jail sentences were intentionally riddled with escape hatches and multiple penalties or "packages" of sentences. Thus, the reality is that "even when 'mandatory' sentences are prescribed, the actual sentence a convicted first [or second] offender receives often depends, to a greater or lesser extent, on the decision [discretion] of the sentencing judge.[10]

Close-up 9.1: Deadliest Drunken Driving Accident in U.S. History

On the night of May 14, 1988, Larry Mahoney drove his pickup truck in the wrong direction down Kentucky Interstate 71 and collided head-on with a school bus carrying 63 children returning

Table 9.1
Changes in Penalties and Requirements for DUI Offenders in Pennsylvania

Convicted Offenders	Old Law	Act 289 (New law)
Fines	$0 to $2,500	$300 to $5,000
Jail	None to 1 year	1st offense = 2 days-2 years 2nd offense = 30 days-2 years 3rd offense = 90 days-2 years Subsequent offense = 1-2 years
License Suspension	1st offense = 6 months 2nd offense = 1 year	One year -
Probation	Permissible	Ineligible
Accelerated Rehabilitation Disposition		
ARD	Permissible, no license suspension required	Permissible for first offenders in most cases, 1 month to 1 year license suspension required
All Offenders		
Evaluation/ Education	Not required	All offenders must be evaluated and attend Alcohol Highway Safety School

Source: The Justice Analyst, October, 1988, Pennsylvania Commission on Crime & Delinquency. Reprinted with permission of Douglas Hoffman

home to Radcliff from a church outing at King's Island amusement park near Cincinnati. Twenty-three children and three adults died from smoke inhalation and burns in the ensuing explosion and fire that engulfed the bus, their bodies charred beyond recognition. Although seriously injured, Mahoney was given a sobriety test in the emergency room two hours after the crash and registered a .24 BAC, over twice the legal limit for DWI in Kentucky.[a] Mahoney admitted that after finishing a 12-hour night shift at the M & T Chemicals plant he had several beers at a local bar and continued drinking later on at a friend's house; the police found a still-cold twelve-pack of Miller Lite in Larry's pickup, with a few cans missing.[b] The state was able to prove that Mahoney had seven beers the night of the accident, while experts estimated that it was closer to twenty-four. It was not the first time that Mahoney was drunk behind the wheel. He plead guilty to DWI in 1984 (.16 BAC), was fined $300, had his license suspended for six months, and was ordered to attend a Driver Alcohol Education Clinic program.[c]

The county prosecutor initially assigned the case had considered seeking the death penalty under a capital murder statute allowing it for reckless conduct resulting in multiple deaths, regardless of intent or motivation, but the special prosecutor[d] who took over declined to do so because of the absence of premeditation. Mahoney was indicted on twenty-seven counts of murder based on conduct "manifesting extreme indifference to human life" in addition to a variety of other related charges.[e] Friends and relatives in Carrollton (Kentucky), where Larry grew up and was known as a "good old boy," raised $540,000 in cash and unencumbered property for Mahoney's bail release from detention in October 1988. And sympathetic community members displayed signs of support ("Larry our prayers are with you") and told TV reporters "Let's tell the truth about it. That could be you or me sitting in that jail. What he done ain't no different than what a whole lot of people in this town or anywhere else have done."[f]

Was it murder, manslaughter, or Ford's fault?

At trial, Mahoney's defense team conceded to the jury that Mahoney was drunk and driving on the wrong side of the road. But they argued[g] it was the faulty design of the 1977-model bus built by Ford Motor Company and not the collision itself—the unprotected gas tank ruptured upon impact, and the seating material was not fire-retardant—that was responsible for the deaths and injuries, not Mahoney. (The autopsies confirmed that it was the fire, not the crash per se, that killed the victims.[h]) Prosecutor Paul Richwalsky emphasized that bus safety was not the issue and that "plain and simple, this is a murder case . . . He killed them just as sure as if he had a gun," but apparently the jury did not see it quite that way. After deliberating eleven hours, Mahoney was found guilty of twenty-seven counts of second-degree manslaughter and virtually all of the remaining counts but was acquitted on the murder charges. Although the jury recommended prison terms totalling over 600 years for all counts combined, because the court imposed concurrent sentences Mahoney was effectively sentenced to sixteen years and is eligible for parole in eight years. The families of the victims were understandably disappointed and embittered with the outcome. "It's always 'Poor Larry Mahoney, he's got to live with this.' But he can see his family. They can visit him. If I want to spend Christmas with my child, I've got to go to the cemetery and kneel down by a headstone."[i]

Mahoney publicly apologized to the families of his victims for the first time during the trial. "I know that you all be wantin' me to say something and tell you I'm sorry and that's what I been wantin' to do but I've been told not to say anything, so I want you to know that I really am sorry . . . It's a fact I was in the accident but I don't remember seein' no bus until after I woke up in the hospital and I was told." Mahoney, who plans to appeal his conviction on twenty-seven counts of second-degree manslaughter, said afterward that he wished he had been locked up for a 1984 drunk driving conviction. "If I'd have stayed 30 days in jail for that first time, I'd never have been back out on that road no more."[j]

[a]*New York Times,* May 22, 1988, p. 6E; *American Bar Association Journal,* September 1, 1988, p. 52.

[b]*People Magazine,* January 8, 1990, p. 53.

[c]*New York Times,* May 17, 1988, p. A16; *USA Today,* May 18, 1988, p. 3A; *American Bar Association Journal,* September 1, 1988, p. 52.

[d]Author's interview with Special Prosecutor Paul W. Richwalsky Jr., February 16, 1990, to clarify inconsistent reports in the literature concerning the state's position on capital murder charges.

[e]Forty-four counts of wanton endangerment, thirteen counts of first-degree assault, one count of drunken driving.

[f]*New York Times,* August 8, 1988, p. A14.

[g]The defense also claimed that Mahoney's intoxication was unintentional because friends had given him a beverage Mahoney did not know was alcohol, but a prosecution witness testified that Mahoney asked for an alcoholic drink just hours before the crash.

[h]*New York Times,* December 21, 1989, p. A28; *New York Times* December 22, 1989, p. A22.

[i]*People,* January 8, 1990, pp. 51-53.

[j]"Inside Edition," WNBC, December 21, 1989.

JUDICIAL RESISTANCE TO MANDATORY SENTENCES

A study revealed that judges in Indiana and New Mexico resisted complying with the mandatory sentence requirements of their states' tough new DWI laws.[11]

The 1983 Indiana law required repeat offenders to serve five days in jail or to complete a minimum of eighty hours of community service, yet fourteen percent of these offenders did neither, and the remaining defendants served or worked less than the mandated time. In addition, the provision that no "good time"[12] could be credited "against the length of a sentence was likewise widely flouted, with some courts actually stating on the jail commitment papers that such credit could be earned."[13] New Mexico's stringent 1984 law required that all second offenders be sent to jail for "not less than 48 consecutive hours which can not be suspended or deferred or taken under advisement."[14] Despite this unequivocal directive, the records showed that "In 30 percent of the cases the judges blatantly failed to give the mandated sentence."[15] Even in those cases where the forty-eight-hour sentence was pronounced, court records verified that only 63 percent of the convicted recidivists actually served the time they were supposed to.[16]

"Although the judges tried to provide some kind of legally valid excuses [for disregarding the law], what seemed to be the case was that they didn't like the law . . . they didn't see why the second offenders needed to be sent to jail."[17] The courts shied away from ordering jail terms because the image of the "killer drunk" embodied in the get-tough statutes did not accord with the typical drunk driving defendants appearing before them on a daily basis—individuals who usually caused no harm, were "merely detected weaving down the highway at midnight on Saturday," and are responsible for just one alcohol-related death for every 330,000 miles driven by drunk drivers.[18]

Wharton Study

A 1984 Wharton School study of the attitudes of 570 trial judges in six states who heard DUI cases revealed what can best be described as judicial ambivalence toward mandatory sentences: "A curious mixture of sentiments in favor of harshness are present at the same time that the traditions in favor of equity and compassion for the unfortunate [drunk drivers] are being expressed."[19] Although a plurality of judges said the "one change" they would make in existing DUI laws would be to "increase the penalties," the sanction they most widely supported was license suspensions, especially for repeat offenders. The judges also endorsed rehabilitative sentences, but very few (20 percent) regarded mandatory sentences as the "most appropriate" disposition for first offenders. The reason for the latter is that the judges believed the existing DUI laws over-emphasized punishment at the expense of rehabilitation. A 1986 study of 79 Minnesota judges also found that judges "disagree about how best to achieve deterrence and rehabilitation" and that even judges in favor of "increased severity" do not necessarily equate that with mandatory sentences.[20] In both studies, judges preferred to impose a "package" of sentences in DUI cases—almost four separate sanctions for both first and second offenders—rather than relying on a single sentence for the typical offender.[21] Judges apparently have difficulty accepting *any* type of mandatory sanctions for drunk drivers, as indicated by an interview with a New Mexico judge who was discussing mandatory license sanctions: "The law was a response to MADD and other pressure groups. The legislature got stampeded. The courts have to resist these pressures."[22]

Weekend Jail

Drunk drivers usually serve their forty-eight-hour jail sentence on the weekend. Weekend jail is used so that incarceration does not interfere with the offender's employment, ability to defray the costs associated with court processing or confinement, or with making restitution when so ordered. Although these statutes defined the mandatory jail period in hours rather than two days, the forty-eight-hour requirement was often circumvented in practice. A ploy used by some corrections departments or jailors to reduce jail overcrowding on the weekends was to equate spending any part of a day in jail as having served the entire day.[23] For example, "At the [New Mexico] city jail very frequently people were admitted at 11:00 o'clock at night and released at 1:00 o'clock the next morning," their "two day" sentence having been completed.[24] To rectify the problem, a number of states have amended their legislation to provide for forty-eight or seventy-two consecutive hours of confinement.

EFFECTIVENESS OF MANDATORY JAIL

With a few isolated exceptions, the research data (so far) provides scant support that mandatory jail sentences are effective in decreasing DUI recidivism, accidents, or fatalities (see Table 9.2).[25] The one notable, much-heralded exception occurred in Hennepin County (Minnesota), which registered a 20 percent decline in nighttime crashes following a mandatory sentence policy for first offenders that was instituted through judicial consensus rather than by legislative fiat. Two years after Hennepin County initiated the program, during which time there was extensive judicial turnover, 82 percent of all first offenders were still being sentenced to two days in jail.[26]

Table 9.2

Selected Findings on the Effectiveness of Mandatory Sentences

Place/Sample	Results
14 state sample	Comparison of 7 states with mandatory penalties (jail, community service, license loss) with 7 states without these severe sanctions. During 1980-1985, drunk driving decline was same for both groups. [a]
Massachusetts	Law has some of the most severe penalties, for both first and multiple offenders, in the country. After four years, about 38% of the defendants arraigned for DUI had been arraigned again for drunk driving. [b]
Wisconsin	The year before the new DWI was passed, drunk drivers caused 413 deaths and contributed to 42% of all highway fatalities, compared to 282 deaths and 34% of the total fatalities two years after the revision. [c]
Maine	Mandatory jail for first offender law had immediate one-year effect of reducing fatal crashes by 33% more than in control states, but by the third year Maine's rate of fatal crashes returned to pre-reform level. [d]
Tennessee	Preliminary results show a large decrease in drunk driving recidivism among first offenders but no significant reduction in alcohol-related accidents. [e]
California	16% reduction in deaths caused by drunk drivers first year (1982) new law was implemented. [f]
Memphis Seattle Cincinnati Hennepin County (Minn.)	National Institute of Justice study found that the 1-2 day mandatory confinement laws in these jurisdictions had no effect on reducing alcohol-related traffic deaths, except in Hennepin county (Minn) where fatalities decreased by 20% in the first five months under the tough new sentencing guidelines, a much larger decrease than in the neighborhing county or for the state as a whole. [g]

[a]Hans C. Joksch, *The Impact of Severe Penalties on Drinking and Driving,* Washington, D.C.: AAA Foundation for Traffic Safety, May 1988.

[b]Carmen A. Cicchetti and Louise A. Enos, *Driving Under The Influence of Liquor: Analysis Four Years After Chapter 373,* Massachusetts Trial Court, June 12, 1987, p. 25.

[c]Lynn S. Adelman, "Introduction" to *Marquette Law Review* special issue on drunken driving 69, no. 2, Winter 1986, 161.

Table 9.2 *(continued)*

[d]Allan R. Meyers et al., "Cops and Drivers: Police Discretion and the Enforcement of Maine's 1981 OUI Law," *Journal of Criminal Justice* 15, no. 5 (1987): 362.
[e]*Drunk Driving Law and Enforcement: An Assessment of Effectiveness,* Washington, D.C.: American Bar Association (Criminal Justice Section), February 1986, p. 90.
[f]*Jailing Drunk Drivers: Impact on the Criminal Justice System,* Washington, D.C.: National Institute of Justice, May 1985 (Executive Summary), pp. 32-33; same title in NIJ Research in Brief, November 1984.
[g]*Jailing Drunk Drivers,* executive summary, pp. 17-31.

Taken as a whole, though, the studies indicate that imposing a forty-eight or seventy-two-hour mandatory jail term is no more of a deterrent than giving drunk drivers fines, suspended sentences, or community service.[27] (Aside from license suspensions, there is little evidence that any sanctions reduce recidivism or traffic accidents.) And whatever initial impact mandatory sentences do have are short-lived and highly dependent on the amount of publicity accorded the new law.[28] Hingson found, for example, that fatal crashes in Maine started to decline even before the passage of the tougher law, which was widely publicized in advance.[29] And Ross notes that increasing the length of mandatory sentences, as the statutes do for repeat offenders, "appears to result in changes that lessen the certainty of its application, which in turn reduce the deterrent effectiveness of the law."[30] Under a 1970 Christmas crackdown on drunk drivers in Chicago that was highly publicized and extended through June 1971, it was decreed that all persons convicted of drinking and driving during that period would automatically receive a seven-day jail sentence. Robertson's evaluation of the crackdown found that Chicago's subsequent fatality rate was not statistically different from a control city where the sentencing of DWI defendants was "business as usual."[31] It was precisely because of the inability to document that mandatory sentences had any effect on highway safety that the American Bar Association came out in opposition to mandatory sentences for first offencers.[32]

Although mandatory sentences do not seem to work, nonetheless "it would be a mistake to reject the use of incarceration on the basis of current evidence."[33] Mandatory confinement represents a recognition of the intrinsic seriousness of the offense itself, may advance other dispositional alternatives, and may have an important role to play in making drinking and driving socially unacceptable

Figure 9.1
Fatal Auto Accidents Reported in Pennsylvania, 1980-1987

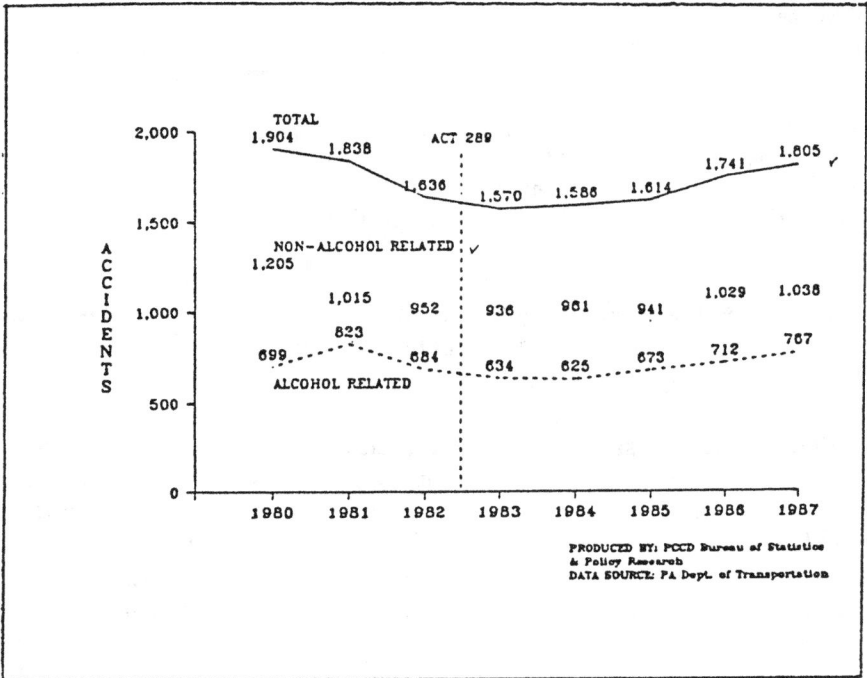

The impact of mandatory-sentence drunk driving laws seems to wane over time. Alcohol-related fatal accidents in Pennsylvania peaked in 1981 at 823. They decreased 17 percent in 1982, the year the new mandatory-sentence law was considered and passed by the legislature, and there was an additional 7 percent decrease in fatalities in 1983, the year the act actually went into effect. However, since 1984, alcohol-related fatal accidents have increased steadily, to 767 in 1987. *Source:* Figure 9.1 from *The Justice Analyst,* October 1988, Pennsylvania Commission on Crime and Delinquency, reprinted with permission of Douglas Hoffman.

behavior—one of the major goals of the President's Commission On Drunk Driving.[34] And because defendants sentenced to jail are probably the more serious DWI offenders, then the fact that incarcerated offenders do no worse than drunk drivers given nonjail sentences may mask the true impact of mandatory jail sentences.[35] In actuality, the effectiveness of mandatory sentences is largely inconclusive because of the infrequency and inconsistency with which they have been applied and carried out.[36]

COMMUNITY SERVICE

Not everyone agrees that incarceration is an appropriate sanction for drunk drivers. There is considerable support for utilizing community service or other alternatives to jail for convicted first offenders. "Although community service is viewed by some to be only a slap on the wrist, it does provide a harsher penalty than is currently being received by the majority of DUI offenders. Instead of the present system of non-punishment, the offender can be punished while at the same time providing restitution to the community."[37]

Most of the (first offender) "mandatory" jail statutes give courts the option of imposing community service in lieu of or in addition to jail; Colorado, Oregon, Utah, and Connecticut to name a few. (The laws in New Mexico and Tennessee are the exception, containing no loopholes watering down mandatory confinement for first offenders.[38]) By 1986, for example, sixteen states had legislation requiring jail or alternative sanctions (usually community service) for the first offender.[39] A few states, such as Florida, make community service a mandatory, though not necessarily exclusive, disposition.[40] The 1983 Presidential Commission on Drunk Driving recommended 100 hours of community service or a jail sentence of 48 consecutive hours, which was also endorsed by Congress in 1984 in Public Law 98-363.[41] By 1987, over twenty states had legislation authorizing this option for first or multiple offenders (see Figure 9.2).[42] While there is much greater consensus that second offenders should be given longer jail terms that are binding, a few jurisdictions are experimenting with "shock-probation" for repeaters—a short jail sentence followed by supervised probation and/or community service.[43]

The preference for community service instead of jail is part of a generic correctional philosophy that advocates, for all offenders, "the development and use of the least restrictive sanctions, punishments, programs, and facilities consistent with public safety and social order . . . Prisons and jails are a scarce and expensive commodity that should be used only for offenders who cannot be safely confined or safely supervised in less restrictive and less costly programs."[44] Because most first offender "drunk drivers are classified as low-risk, non-violent offenders who have no prior criminal history," many correctional authorities consider community service or other jail alternatives to be the most appropriate sentence for this group. At a cost of $43,000 per bed to build a new jail and $9,500-17,000 a year to maintain an inmate in jail, community service, pragmatic treatment programs, intensive probation and the like are a

Figure 9.2
States with Community Service in Lieu of Jail (As of January 1, 1985)

Community service in lieu of jail for first DWI offense
(Hours; 8 hours = 1 day)

Community service in lieu of jail for second DWI offense
(Days; 1 day = 8 hours of community service work)

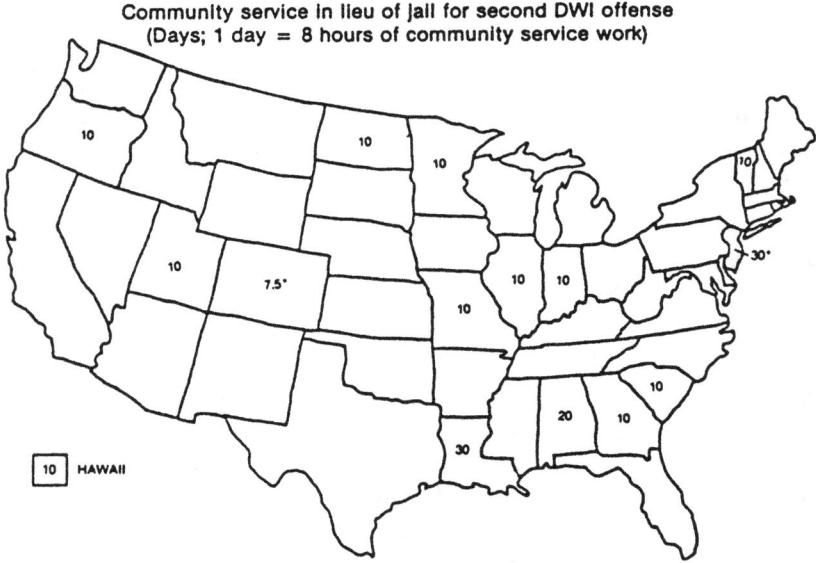

*Community service sentence mandatory (not in lieu of jail)
Source: National Highway Traffic Safety Administration, 1985

Some correctional authorities consider community service more appropriate than jail, particularly for first-offender drunk drivers. By 1987, over twenty states had statutes authorizing community service for first or second DWI offenders.

desperately needed, cost-effective means (see Figure 9.3) for alleviating jail overcrowding—overcrowding that has been exacerbated by "hard" mandatory sentences for second DUI offenders.[45]

Mandatory jail for second offenders is more likely to mean just that, but some states allow judges to waive or suspend incarceration if the defendant enrolls in a rehabilitation program. For example, Massachusetts provides "mandatory" incarceration of seven days to two years for second offenders. But if the judge believes that incarceration would be inappropriate, the offender may instead be sentenced to fourteen days in a residential alcohol treatment program, probation and thirty hours of community service.[46] California's 1982 "mandatory" two- to four-day jail sentence, applicable to almost all convicted drunk drivers, can be avoided by participating in the state's Drinking Driver Program for a year of treatment/education and assuming the program costs of $650.[47]

Figure 9.3
Estimated Annual Cost vs. Benefits for Baton Rouge, Louisiana, Community Service Program (January 1-December 31, 1983)

Program Area	No. of Successful Clients	No. of Hours Worked	Est. Value of Work Performed	Averted Jail ** Costs	Estimated Program Costs
Litter Detail	521	16,672	$55,851.20*	$19,537.50	$21,398.74
Community Service	1,253	41,383	221,966.19	46,987.50	26,388.18
Total	1,774	58,055	$277,817.39	$66,525.00	$47,786.92

*Minimum wage = $3.35
**Averted jail costs = $18.75 × 2 days per client

Source: Baton Rouge City Court, 1984

At a cost of $43,000 per bed to build a new jail and at least $10,000 a year to maintain an inmate in jail, community service is an attractive and cost-effective alternative to mandatory sentences for many DWI offenders.

10

Impact of Mandatory Sentences on the Criminal Justice System

CONSEQUENCES OF MANDATORY SENTENCES

The National Institute of Justice study, mentioned in Table 9.2, also examined what impact mandatory sentences had on the operation of criminal justice agencies in the four test-site jurisdictions. The NIJ findings, supplemented by results from other states, make clear that mandatory sentences have numerous adverse side effects, deplete the limited resources of the justice system, and may well be counter productive, even in the short run. For example, Purdue University economist John Umbeck found that after Ohio passed a tough drunk driving law, hit-and-run accidents caused by intoxicated drivers rose by 8 percent. The stiffer penalities in that state caused more drunken drivers to flee the scene of an accident because "The higher the penalty for drunk driving, the more there is to gain by leaving the scene."[1] The main systemwide consequences of mandatory sentences may be summarized as follows.[2]

• An increase in arrests (33 percent in Seattle), possibly because the police had greater motivation to enforce drunk driving laws expecting that offenders would no longer be able to get off with a slap on the wrist. A study found that police in Kentucky became more aggressive in DUI enforcement under the state's new tough drunk driving law.[3]

11

Non-Cruel and Unusual Punishment

IGNITION INTERLOCKS

An ingenious preventive drunk driving innovation is the ignition interlock system, a technology that can prevent alcohol-impaired drivers from starting their cars. The driver blows into a hand-held breath analyzer (see photo 11.1) that is linked to a microprocessor in a small ignition-locking device under the dashboard. If the driver does not use or pass the BAC test, the car will not start.[1] Each interlock system can be selectively programmed to set the pass/fail BAC reading at any level. Most places using interlock sentences for convicted offenders require absolute sobriety (0.00 BAC), while others have set the interlock at more than one beer or at .05 BAC.[2] In California, which adopted statewide use of the interlock system in September 1986, the ignition will not work if the BAC is above .03.[3]

In December 1988, New York became the eleventh state to pass a law promoting the use of "interlock sentences" as a condition of probation or (less often) of license restoration; and thirty states introduced interlock legislation in their 1989 legislative sessions.[4] The system is so promising that over 200 judges around the country, acting pursuant to the enabling legislation or on their own authority, are ordering convicted drunk drivers—particularly repeat offenders and first offenders with very high BACs—to have the ignition inter-

• A substantial increase in not-guilty pleas and requests for jury trials. The latter doubled at first in Seattle and increased by 33 percent in California.[4] Not-guilty pleas increased from 27 percent to 74 percent in Phoenix, Arizona.[5]

• Dismissals increased. After Washington state mandated a one-day jail sentence for first DWI ofenders in 1983, "the district courts were in a state of crisis, a large number of DWI defendants were having their charges reduced or dismissed, and the 'tough' new DWI penalties were therefore being infrequently applied."[6]

• Incarceration rates and jail overcrowding increased dramatically.

• Conviction rates decreased, although not uniformly so.[7]

Heaviest Toll on Courts and Corrections

Mandatory confinement takes its greatest toll on the courts and especially on corrections departments. In order to contain court case-loads in Seattle, the number of deferred prosecutions—a practice that the President's Commission recommended eliminating—increased from a negligible 1.5 percent in 1979 to over 12 percent in 1982.[8] Because of heavy jail backlogs in Cincinnati and Memphis, first offenders had to wait up to seven months before starting to serve their weekend sentences. In Pennsylvania, DUI commitments to county jails skyrocked from 1,055 the year before the new law year to 9,287 in 1987 (see Figure 10.1), and increased by 1,300 percent since 1981.[9] When the King County daily jail population rose from 836 in 1979 to 1,047 in 1982, a new facility had to be opened to handle all of the first offenders. Mandatory sentences can become a nightmare for probation departments because some of the laws (like Tennessee's) require all convicted drunk drivers to be placed on probation, besides any other sanction that might be imposed. Severe disruptions in the machinery of justice that cause havoc, however, are not an inevitable outcome of mandatory sentences. The Minnesota experience demon-strated that mandatory confinement can be implemented "without causing problems for the police, courts, or incarceration facilities."[10] For example, the courts in Hennepin County adopted a flexible range of measures to handle the law's anticipated impact on corrections, such as immediate incarceration upon conviction in order to avoid peaks in weekend jail populations, and requiring offenders to defray the costs of their confinement and treatment programs.

Figure 10.1
Sentenced DUI Admissions to County Jails, 1981-1987

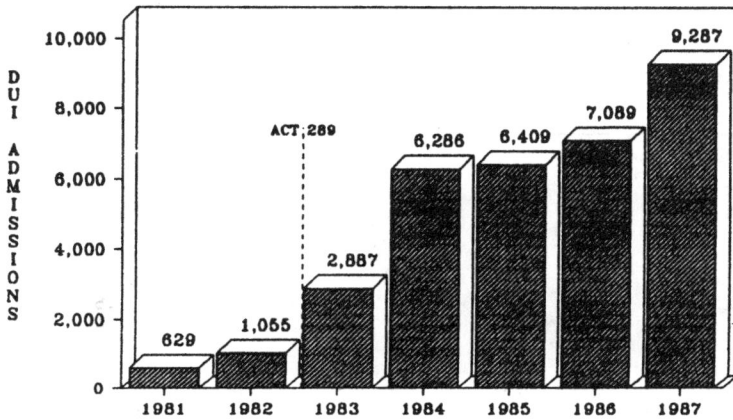

Produced by: PCCD Bureau of Statistics & Policy Research
Data Source: Pa. Dept. of Corrections

Mandatory sentences take the greatest toll on correctional facilities. In Pennsylvania, DUI commitments to county jails skyrocketed from 1,055 the year before the new law to 9,287 in 1987.

Making Offenders Pay for Crime

The Presidential Commission on Drunk Driving recommended that drunk drivers should defray the costs incurred by the state in connection with their arrest, incarceration, and treatment, a suggestion being implemented in some jurisdictions. John Klein, for example, a twenty-seven-year-old third-time offender, was given the choice of spending one year in jail or doing thirty days in the Glenwood jail in Akron (Ohio), undergoing alcohol therapy and reimbursing the state $370. Michael Faverty, another prisoner at the same facility, pays $862 for his thirty-day jail sentence as an out-of-state resident. In 1986 California's Sen. Edward Royce sponsored a law that made persons who drive under the influence of alcohol or drugs liable for the costs of "any incident" that results in an "emergency response." Starting in 1988 that law, interpreted broadly, was used by the city of San Jose to bill drunk driving suspects for police time associated with their arrest even if they are not convicted of the offense.[11]

Table 10.1
Profile of Jail Inmates Convicted or Charged with DWI, 1983

Characteristic	% of inmates
Sex	
Male	94.7
Female	5.3
Race	
White	85.6
Black	9.8
Other	4.6
Ethnicity	
Hispanic	17.2
Non-Hispanic	82.8
Age	
17-19 years	2.4
20-24	22.3
25-29	17.3
30-34	17.1
35-39	11.6
40-44	8.0
45-49	6.9
50-54	6.8
55-64	6.5
65 and older	1.0
Median age	32 years
Education	
Less than 8 years	13.1
8-9	15.9
10-11	19.4
12	36.0
Some college	15.7
Median education	12 years
Marital Status	
Married	22.2
Widowed	2.0
Divorced/separated	39.1
Never married	36.7
Employment status at arrest	
Unemployed	32.7
Employed	67.3
Full-time	58.2
Part-time	9.1

Source: Lawrence A. Greenfield, Drunk Driving, *Bureau of Justice Statistics Special Report,* February 1988, p. 4.

SPECIAL CORRECTIONAL FACILITIES FOR
DRUNK DRIVERS

In response to mandatory-sentence overcrowding, some jurisdictions have established special jails designated solely for repeat
offenders who have not injured anyone while DUI, where the
emphasis is upon treatment programs that are usually provided by
outside contractors.

When the proportion of DUI offenders committed to county jails
in Massachusetts reached 25 percent due to the state's tough new
Drunk Driving Law, Massachusetts opened the Longwood Treatment Center in May 1985, "the state's first minimum security prison
designed exclusively to detain and provide alcoholism education and
treatment to multiple drunken driving offenders."[12] The 125-bed
facility, located in a residential neighborhood of Boston, purchases
its treatment services from Valle Associates and is staffed by
uniformed corrections officers twenty-four hours a day. "It is
important to stress that the facility is secure, and therefore the
paramount objective of the Department of Correction at the facility
is the detention of multiple drunk driving offenders. The secondary
objective is the treatment of alcoholism."[13] Compared to depart-
mentwide recidivism (25 percent) and at other low-security
institutions (19 percent), only 6 percent of the Longwood completers
had been rearrested and incarcerated for more than thirty days within
a year of their release.

In Connecticut, men convicted of DWI at least twice may be sent
to the D.W.I. Unit at Camp Hartell in Windsor Locks, for a period
of forty-eight hours up to six months. The 100-bed minimum security
"prison," opened in May 1987 on the grounds of the National Guard
barracks, has carpeted buildings in which the inmates live, the
grounds are landscaped with flower beds, and the men are not
required to wear uniforms. "The department recognizes they are not
serious criminals. The main emphasis here at Hartell/D.W.I. is on
treatment." Since Hartell opened in 1987, about 5,000 drunk drivers
have passed through the facility, about 14 percent of whom have
been returned to Hartell or other prisons for the same offense. The
centerpiece of the Hartell program, for all inmates, is Alcoholics
Anonymous therapy. Half of the inmates sent to Hartell each year
stay there for less than ten days. And because of persistent overcrowding, even inmates sentenced to thirty days may stay only
seventy-two hours before being placed on supervised release.[14] A

second D.W.I. Unit was opened in Middleton on the grounds of the Connecticut Valley Hospital a year later because "treating these offenders in a setting away from the general inmate population is likely to improve their chances for a successful return to the community and lessen the likelihood of a repeat offense."[15]

Drunk drivers in Akron (Ohio) are diverted from the overcrowded county jail—under a longstanding court order not to exceed 186 prisoners—to a special lockup opened in May 1989, located in a converted school building where they are guarded by sheriff's deputies, receive remedial therapy from a private contractor, and must reimburse the county for at least part of the cost of incarceration, besides any fines imposed. The inmates' daily routine consists of eight hours of classes, lectures, and group therapy. Of approximately 115 people who completed their sentences, none has been reincarcerated.[16]

In places like Washington County (Maryland), drunk drivers may be allowed to complete a forty-eight-hour sentence in a detoxification center on the weekend, and offenders serving time in regular jails are, whenever possible, kept separate from the rest of the more "prison-wise" inmate population.[17]

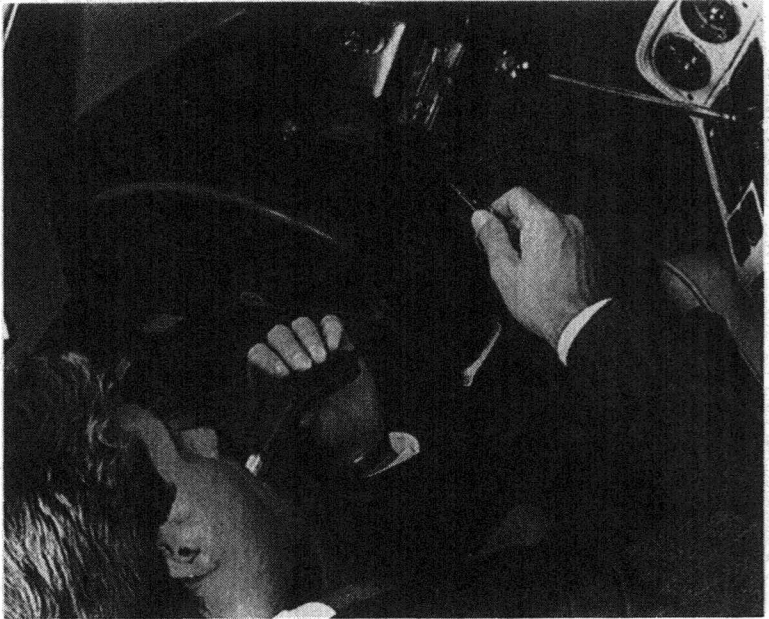

Photo 11.1
Ignition Interlock Device

Drunkproofing cars with ignition interlock system: "It is now possible to develop a nearly foolproof device that will prevent an alcohol impaired driver from starting his car." The driver blows into a handheld unit, which transmits electrical impulses to the control model mounted on dashboard of car. The present main application of the device, marketed by Guardian Interlock (Denver, Colo.) and Safety Interlock (Carmel, Calif.) is to monitor and control the behavior of high-risk convicted drunk drivers on probation. The manufacturers also plan to market the system to families with teenage drivers—as part of a Responsible Driver Program—and to owners of commercial fleets of trucks, buses, and taxis. Will ignition interlocks make sobriety checkpoints obsolete? Photos courtesy of Dr. Donald W. Collier/Guardian Technologies Inc.

lock system installed at their own expense as a condition of probation.[5] In Calvert County (Maryland), for example, Judge Larry Lamson orders interlocks for first offenders with .15 BACs or more at the time of arrest, and for repeat offenders with .08 BACs or more.[6] Even before the New York law was passed, a village justice in Adams ordered a fifty-four-year-old repeat offender to install interlock in his auto for the period of his three-year probation, the first such sentence in the state.[7] Some courts utilize interlock sentences primarily as an alternative to jail, community service, or license suspensions (e.g., California), while others view it as a device to augment rather than replace such sentencing options.[8] First offenders in Cumberland County (Pennsylvania) are encouraged to rent the system in return for a reduction in their license suspension from six months to just one month.[9] A distict advantage of interlock sentences is that they do not interfere with the probationer's employment or going for treatment, and they make license suspensions unnecessary, which sentencing judges recognize are commonly disregarded.[10]

Safeguards incorporated into the interlock program make it difficult for someone else to blow into the breath analyzer or for the offender to tamper with the equipment. User-identification codes must be verified by the system's computer, which also maintains a log of the driver's breath test readings and has an electronic memory that records any attempts at tampering. As part of the interlock-probation sentence, offenders must take their vehicle to the manufacturer's service station for periodic inspections[11] to verify that the system is working properly and has not been tampered with.[12] Moreover, "It is awfully hard to get a sober person to blow into a machine to let a drunk driver drive [and] they are taking on some real liability if they do that."[13] Any such irregularities are promptly reported by the manufacturer to the sentencing court, constitute a violation of probation, and can result in a thirty-to sixty-day jail term and $500 fine.[14] In some states there are special marks on the license plate of interlock equipped vehicles to alert police to the special status of the driver.[15]

Ignition interlocks have been endorsed not only by the criminal justice community but by the users themselves. "It was a godsend for me," said a twenty-eight-year old sales manager in Carlyle (Pennsylvania) who was put on interlock for a year.[16] The most common reaction from probationers has been, "I can't lie to this device. It makes me stop and realize if I'm going to drink, I'm not going to drive."[17] The reason that the interlock system is such a powerful behavior modification tool is because it provides direct feedback and an immediate sanction—perceived as severe punishment by the offenders—which is not dependent on the driver being stopped and arrested by the police. Studies show that jurisdictions using interlock sentences have reduced the number of repeat drunk driving offenses in their jurisdictions by an average of seventy percent more than those that do not.[18] A study conducted jointly by the Hamilton County Municipal Court (Cincinnati) and the University of Colorado in July 1987 found that of the 231 offenders using interlocks only 1.3 percent were rearrested for DUI in the eight-month follow-up period, compared to 9.2 percent rearrests for the 1,918 nonuser offenders. High praise for ignition interlocks came from no less an authority in the field than Donald Nichols, editor of the *Drinking/Driving Law Letter:* "That's the only thing I've seen that has any real chance of working."[19]

MORGUE TOUR

Compulsory morgue visits[20] introduced in 1985, especially for first offenders, are becoming a routine procedure in California, where at least twenty-four judges throughout the state have ordered such visits (besides any other penalties) as part of a 1988 state law officially endorsing this practice. In order to stress graphically the destructive nature of drinking and driving to youthful offenders, a 1989 amendment allowed persons under eighteen convicted of drunk driving to be sentenced, at the court's discretion, to visit coroners' offices "where they can witness the effects of their behavior firsthand."[21] The morgue visits were legislatively expanded to youthful offenders because the fifteen- to twenty-year-old group makes up only 8 percent of the nation's population but accounts for 17 percent of the drivers involved in alcohol-related fatalities.[22] Sacramento Superior Court Judge Jeffrey Gunther has attracted national attention and recognition for his morgue tour sentences. In addition to conditions of probation that may include restitution, fines, and serving two days in the county jail, Judge Gunther imposes the following terms on eighteen- to twenty-one-year-olds who are convicted of drunk driving:

• Visit the emergency room of the Sacramento Medical Center between 10 P.M. and 2 A.M. on a Friday or Saturday night to observe the victims of auto accidents involving the drinking driver. In addition, a tour of the hospital's Acute Care Clinic for alcoholics in the terminal stages of their disease is provided.

• Visit the county coroner's office to observe victims of alcohol-related auto fatalities.

• At the conclusion of these visits, a personal meeting takes place with the young offenders and their attorney and/or parents in Judge Gunther's chambers to discuss the youths' reactions to the experiences and what impact it will have on future conduct.[23]

Intended to both shock and impress offenders with the fraility of human life, only 6 of the over 400 youthful offenders given this special sentence were rearrested for drunk driving. "I wouldn't even run a red light now much less drink and drive," said a young man who participated in the monthly tour of the Orange County coroner's office. A similar program went into effect in Des Moines in December 1988, New York has been using them for some time, and judges in other states have sentenced adult offenders to work in morgues or hospital emergency rooms as part of a community service sentence.[24]

OTHER CREATIVE SENTENCES

In Texas, authorities can seize the cars of drunken drivers with at least four convictions under the vehicle forfeiture provision of the state's drunk driving laws. Brooklyn district attorney Elizabeth Holtzman announced that her office would seize the automobiles of repeat offenders and drunk drivers who cause death or serious injury under the state's new (1984) Civil Forfeiture Law, a RICO-type statute whose major thrust is to combat drug trafficking and racketeering. "Paying fines often is no deterrent. Taking a car will be."[25] Drivers convicted of drunk driving in Judge Jeffrey Ford's courtroom (Urbana, Illinois) faced a controversial new sentence (not authorized by statute) starting in early 1988: placing an ad in their local newspaper, complete with a photo and vital statistics, publicly apologizing for their violation "If you keep the DWI matter in the public eye, then it should have some impact."[26] County Judge Becky Titus in Sarasota (Florida) orders first offenders to display a bumper sticker on their cars identifying them as convicted drunk drivers.[27] And a Pennsylvania legislator proposed a modern-day "scarlet letter" sentence that would stigmatize offenders by having them display a special red license plate identifying them as convicted drunk drivers.[28]

Elsewhere, drunk drivers have been sentenced to house arrest, listening to a tape recording (with the sounds of screaming children) made of the accident they caused,[29] giving talks to civic groups about their experience with drunken driving (the driver in question was released after serving one month of a 20-year sentence),[30] and writing essays on why not to speed. After pleading guilty to manslaughter (.23 BAC), M. Norvel Young, chancellor of Pepperdine University, was able to avoid going to jail for a year by doing a research project on the relationship between stress among ''high-effective'' businessmen and alcohol-related accidents.[31] That should teach the distinguished scholar a lesson!

12

Third Party Liability for Alcohol-Related Accidents

COMMERCIAL SERVERS

Those victimized by drunk drivers are filing a record number of suits against commercial servers of alcohol—bartenders, restaurant and tavern owners, table servers—and are being awarded substantial damages against these third parties for selling drinks to customers who kill or injure someone in a DWI accident after leaving their establishments. The legal grounds on which third-party liability[1] has been established are existing state laws that apply specifically to commercial servers of alcoholic beverages (dram shop acts) and the doctrine of negligence.

Dram Shop Acts

At common law, tavern owners and bartenders were immune from liability for the injuries caused by intoxicated patrons, because the consumption of alcohol and not the serving of it was considered the proximate cause of the injuries.[2] At that time, it was an unquestioned axiom that innkeepers were not their patrons' keepers. Starting in the mid-1850s under the impetus of the Prohibition movement, some states rejected the common law nonliability rule by enacting dram shop (civil damages) acts that expressly imposed liability on the owners and operators of drinking establishments.[3] Reflecting changing concepts of causation, these dram shop statutes held licensed servers liable for injuries incurred directly after serving liquor to intoxicated patrons, on the revised belief that the act of furnishing the alcohol was the proximate cause of the injuries or death. The 1853 Indiana dram shop act, the prototype for fourteen states that currently also have dram shop acts on their books, provided that anyone injured by an intoxicated individual had the right to seek damages against any person "who shall by retailing spiritous liquor have caused the intoxication of such person."[4] Vendor liability is now generally predicated on establishing that alcohol was served to a customer who was "obviously" or "visibly intoxicated," or to a minor.[5] (In many states, the driver's license of persons younger than 21 is stamped with a "Y" for Youth, or with an "Under 21" next to their photo to alert commercial servers to their underage drinking status.)

Liability Based On Negligence Theory

Absent dram shop legislation, starting in the mid-1950s, judges in a growing number of states took the position that the common law nonliability dictum "may be abrogated by the courts when the mores have so changed that perpetuation of the rule would do violence to the social conscience."[6] Basically these courts utilized negligence principles as the rationale and legal framework for imposing DWI liability on vendors: Service personnel have a special relationship with their customers and a duty to protect the public from the danger posed by overindulgent patrons. The harmful consequences of excessive drinking are or should be reasonably foreseeable. Servers breach that duty when they sell drinks to visibly intoxicated individuals or otherwise fail to adhere to a proper standard of care in dispensing alcohol. The vendor is therefore considered responsible for the occurrence (the proximate cause) of the DWI accident and liable for the injuries sustained by the victim.[7]

Proliferation of Liability Suits

Under the auspices of dram shop acts or negligence doctrine, by 1987 over thirty-seven states had adopted some type of liability for licensed servers, with entirely predictable results.[8] Dram shop DUI liability cases are growing at the phenomenal rate of 300 percent a year and have tripled between 1982 and 1985.[9] As many as 3,000 liability cases were filed against all servers in 1985 alone, with the typical case involving awards in excess of $100,000.[10] In 1985 a Morgan County (Indiana) jury brought in a $10.3 million judgment against the Brown County Inn for medical costs and suffering in the case of Katherine Smock, who was permanently brain damaged after a head-on collision with a drunk driver (.25 BAC) who had been drinking for at least five hours at the inn before the accident. "The evidence was quite strong" that the bartender knew that Jackson was intoxicated but continued to serve him nonetheless.[11]

Liability Insurance Crisis

Because of the dramatic rise in successful dram shop suits and escalating judgments, the costs of obtaining liability insurance have soared or become unaffordable; and in some areas insurance companies have dropped vendor liability coverage altogether.[12] An estimated 50-60 percent of the 8,000-10,000 taverns and restaurants in New Jersey no longer have liability coverage.[13] Liability insurance rates for the Melody Bar (New Brunswick, New Jersey) went from $1,500 in 1981 to $20,000 in 1988—a 1,200 percent increase. To discourage customers from driving while intoxicated, the owners hung a large painting of a car sideswiping a truck on the wall with the message "Don't Drink and Drive" on it. The sign was so successful that it drove customers away. A bar owner in Washington, D.C., found that his premiums jumped from $185 in 1984 to $26,500 the next year, for half the amount of coverage.[14]

BATTLE BREWING OVER VENDOR LIABILITY

Reducing Exposure to Liability

There is an emerging trend toward limiting vendor liability in response to the insurance crisis and as a reprimand to judges who have taken it upon themselves to broaden DUI liability without legislative approval. In 1986 alone, legislatures in nineteen states, often at the urging of the liquor industry, enacted new laws or amended existing dram shop acts to limit commercial server or social host liability in one way or another.[15]

Commercial servers claim that the "visibly intoxicated" standard is too amorphous to expose then to the risk of liability, and is merely used to make them a deep-pocket scapegoat for displaced responsibility. In some parts of the country vendors are lobbying for statutory changes that would lower their threshold of liability by requiring that the patron be legally rather than visibly intoxicated.[16] And some bars have installed breath-testing devices that persons suspected of being (or before becoming) visibly intoxicated must pass before the bartender will continue to serve them.[17] The two most common steps taken to limit liability is legislation that would place a statutory ceiling on the amount of damages that may be recovered from dram shop defendants, and self-monitoring "responsible server" programs undertaken by the vendors themselves. Connecticut limits damages to $50,000 per incident, and Maine sets the cap at $250,000 per defendant, while other states may have ceilings as high as $500,000 per lawsuit.[18]

Server Training Programs

Various programs around the country emphasize server training as the key to avoiding liability or minimizing damages. TIPS,[19] a front-runner in this area, is a "program to train purveyors of alcohol to recognize signs of impending intoxication. They can intervene before the person gets behind the wheel of a car and prevent the problem from occurring."[20] Creating a responsible drinking environment is accomplished through a program involving slide presentations, videotaped vignettes, role-playing exercises, and server skills and sensitivity training. Service establishments that pass an examination at the end of the workshop and maintain responsible drinking practices are awarded three-year certification, which may be introduced as part of a "best efforts" defense in a negligence liability suit.[21] Under Oregon's first-of-a-kind "server education law," satisfactory completion of a server training program or certification can be used by tavern owners to immunize them from, restrict the scope of, or constitute a defense to third-party negligence.[22] As a defense to liability, Maine's Liquor Liability Act permits defendants to offer proof that they adhered to "responsible serving practices"— as evidenced by training programs that teach bartenders how to spot intoxicated customers or how to refuse serving any patron who appears to have had one too many—or that they followed other responsible management policies, procedures and actions, such as eliminating happy hours.[23]

Photo 12.1
Breath-Testing Machines in Bars

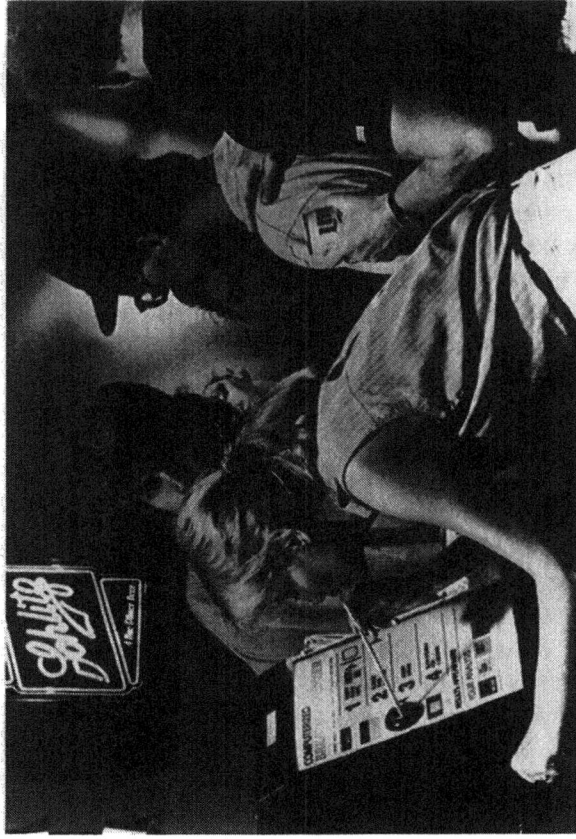

As a precaution against liability suits, some bars have installed breath testing devices which patrons suspected of being, or before becoming, "visibly intoxicated" must pass before the bartender will continue to serve them. One such device, designed by Rodger, is operating in the Snuggery Restaurant in Mount Prospect (Ill.) where, for 25 cents, the patron uses a straw to provide a breath sample, and the Computerized Breath Analyzer provides a visual and verbal readout of the alcohol level. Photo courtesy of Communidyne, Inc., Northbrook, IL 60062. Myskyns Tavern (Charleston, S.C.) has a "Sniffer" apparatus breath analyzer, developed by Sam Gasque, head of Know When Corp. To use the Sniffer, a customer simply picks up the telephone receiver as though making a call, follows the verbal instructions heard in the handset, and counts to ten. The results are provided both verbally and on a small screen on top of the unit. The Sniffer shown is telling the user, "Warning, you are legally intoxicated. Do not drive." Photo courtesy of Sam Gasque/Know When.

Responsible Beverage Service Project

The Margaritaville restaurant in Capitola (California) was one of six taverns in the Santa Cruz and Monterey areas participating in a two-year federally funded server training study. The Responsible Beverage Service Project taught bartenders, table servers, and managers about the inhibitory effects of alcohol on motor responses, how servers can detect and assess a customer's condition, and techniques for slowing down a patron's drinking. "We train servers to intervene before a drinker becomes intoxicated, beginning when a guest enters the establishment and the server has an opportunity to make a good impression."[24] A smaller project at a San Diego Navy Club reduced the number of intoxicated patrons by 45 percent through the simple expedient of no longer serving beer by the pitcher.[25]

SOCIAL HOST LIABILITY

Mr. and Mrs. Social Host were throwing a cookout attended by several friends. Nancy Guest was drinking large quantities of beer at the cookout, had spilled beer on one of the hosts, and was obviously drunk, yet the Hosts continued to serve her. As Nancy drove away from the party her van flipped over and killed one of the guests. Should the victim's family be able to sue the Hosts? Why? There has been an attempt, in recent years, to extend vicarious liability to private individuals (social hosts) who serve alcohol to intoxicated guests who injure someone in a traffic accident after leaving the host's home, party, or social gathering.

Legal Grounds for Host Liability

Courts recognizing social host liability have done so primarily on the basis of the same negligence principles that apply to and trigger liability for vendors: When a private party serves alcohol to visibly intoxicated guests who will be driving shortly, "the danger of ultimate harm is as equally foreseeable to the . . . social host as to the bartender," and "is equally as great, regardless of the source of the liquor"—thereby making the host the proximate cause of the injuries sustained.[26] Some courts have found a cause of action against social hosts in dram shop acts whose broad statutory language can be construed as covering social hosts as well as vendors who pour one too many for their guests: "It is unlawful for a person to sell, barter, deliver or *give away* [emphasis mine] an alcoholic beverage to another person who is in a state of intoxication."[27] And all states have Alcoholic Beverage Control acts that typically prohibit anyone from furnishing alcohol to minors because they "pose a potentially high risk of danger to the general public" and "as a class are simply incompetent to deal responsibly with the effects of alcohol."[28] These liquor control acts are especially well suited for imposing liability on hosts who serve alcohol to minor guests who injure someone in an auto accident after leaving the host's premises.

Kelly v. Gwinnell

In an unprecedented decision in *Kelly* v. *Gwinnell* (1984), the New Jersey Supreme Court extended liability to social hosts for injuries stemming from the traffic accident of an intoxicated *adult* guest.[29] Donald Gwinnell (.28 BAC) had a head-on collision after leaving the home of friends who had served him about thirteen drinks in the course of an hour. The Court announced that an injured victim could sue a social host on the grounds of negligence "where the social host directly serves[30] the drunken guest and continues to do so even after the guest is visibly intoxicated, knowing that the guest will soon be driving home."[31] While acknowledging that the decision might put somewhat of a damper on the enjoyment that accompanies social gatherings, it felt that "just compensation to the victims of drunken driving as well as the added deterrent effect of the rule on such driving outweigh the importance of those other values."

Legislatures Curtail Host Liability

Expressing their disagreement with the *Kelly* decision and ire over the court's "overreaching," in 1986 the New Jersey legislature passed new laws to reduce social host liability in connection with intoxicated guests who later injure victims in auto mishaps. Under the new statutory standards for determining liability, the guest must be visibly intoxicated in the host's presence and under circumstances manifesting "reckless disregard of the consequences" to the life and property of another. If the guest has a BAC of less than .15, the social host is presumed to be free of liability; but above .15 the door is wide open for social host liability.[32]

Several state supreme courts, before and after *Kelly*, had imposed liability on social hosts. But these decisions usually applied to hosts who served alcohol to minors, and they were based on broadly worded state dram shop or on liquor control acts. Even then, the state legislatures often acted swiftly to pass laws abrogating these rulings (see Table 12.1). The California Supreme Court recognized a cause of action against the owner of an apartment complex who allegedly served "extremely large amounts of alcohol" to an intoxicated adult guest, knowing that the guest had a history of excessive drinking and was going to drive home. Within months of that decision, the California legislature revised its liquor control act to read: No person who sells or gives away any alcoholic beverage "shall be civilly liable to any injured person" for such injuries "as a result of intoxication by the consumer of such alcoholic beverage."[33] This amendment reinstated the common law nonliability rule immunizing both social hosts and vendors, except when the guest served is a minor.[34] The Wisconsin state legislature took identical action in November 1985.[35]

Future of Host Liability Uncertain

Whatever trend toward host liability the *Kelly* decision may have sparked has apparently been stifled by legislatures that are adamantly opposed to the idea (especially for adult guests) and have effectively overturned the leading cases in the area.[36] Only eleven states have imposed statutory liability on social hosts, while sixteen states have explictly stated that hosts are not liable for third-party injuries.[37] Courts in only a handful of jurisdictions have issued decisions supporting host liability, the effects of which are often tempered by language narrowing the circumstances under which hosts are actually liable and making the extent of such liability unclear.[38] More courts than not have simply refused to impose host liability because it represents "such a fundamental change" in the common law nonliability rule that the issue "is best left to the legislature."[39] Other considerations behind this judicial hands-off position are that widespread host liability "would open up the floodgates of litigation" in every private social drinking situation where someone was injured, would place on every citizen "who pours a drink for a friend a heavy burden to monitor and regulate guests," and because it is patently unfair to hold private parties to the same standard of care and liability as those public places that dispense alcohol as a business.[40]

Table 12.1

Selected Examples of Legislatures Overriding Court Decisions Imposing Social Host Liability

State Supreme Ct.	Court Holding	Legislative Action
Oregon	Found fraternity liable for allowing large quantities of beer to be served to minor who injured someone while driving home.	Passed law diluting court's holding.
Minnesota	Construed broadly-written dram shop act "as imposing civil liability on social hosts as well as commercial providers of alcohol.	Amended dram shop act by deleting reference to "giving" alcohol, thus exempt-social hosts from liability.
Iowa	Recognized cause of action against hosts who serve alcohol to intoxicated minors, based on broadly-worded dram shop act.	Amended dram shop act making it applicable only to licensed servers.
Cal.	Recognized host liability against owner of apartment complex who served adult guest with known drinking problem large amounts of alcohol.	Amended liquor control act so as to revert to common law nonliability rule for hosts and vendors.

Source: Carla K. Smith, "Social Host Liability for Injuries Caused by the Acts of an Intoxicated Guest," *North Dakota Law Review* 59, no. 3 (1983): 456-458, 462-464, 471-472; Derry D. Sparlin, "Social Host Liability for Guests Who Drink and Drive: A Closer Look at the Benefits and the Burdens," *William & Mary Law Review* 27, no. 3 (Spring 1986): 604; Deborah B. Goldberg, "Imposition of Liability on Social Hosts in Drunk Driving Cases: A Judicial Response Mandated by Principles of Common Law and Common Sense," *Marquette Law Review* 69, no. 2 (Winter 1986): 256.

13

Deterring Drunk Driving

GENERAL DETERRENCE

The current approach taken to stem the tide of drunk driving is based on deterrence, as expressed in the variety of countermeasures discussed throughout this book. Is this crackdown on drunk driving working?

General deterrence refers to the impact of the new or strengthened drunk driving laws and related interventions on the driving behavior of the total (general) motoring population, and is typically measured by the number of alcohol-related fatalities. After four years of steady decline (11 percent) from 1982 to 1985, in 1986 the number of alcohol-related fatalities jumped to 24,000, a 7 percent increase over the previous year.[1] The 1986 reversal was particularly noticeable among adolescents: after dropping by 48 percent from 1980 to 1985, the number of deaths of legally intoxicated fifteen- to nineteen- year-old drivers increased by 9 percent in 1986 from the prior year.[2] Fatal single-vehicle nighttime crashes—considered the most reliable barometer of drunk driving—increased 7 percent in 1986 over 1985 for all age groups combined, after dropping 20 percent from 1980 to 1985. Single-vehicle nighttime fatalities among fifteen- to nineteen-year-olds evidenced a similar pattern of decline followed by a dramatic upswing (17 percent increase) in 1986.[3]

These statistics, however, may not reflect completely the status of the deterrent response to drunk driving. In a poll by the Roper organization, the number of respondents who said they drove after drinking dropped from 37 percent in 1985 to 28 percent in 1988. Among those who admitted to drinking and driving less, 36 percent said it was because of their awareness of the tougher laws and fines.[4] Statistics compiled by the Insurance Institute for Highway Safety showed that the proportion of fatally injured drivers who were legally drunk dropped from 50 percent in 1982 to 40 percent in 1987.[5] Moreover, "Simply showing that the level of blood alcohol among [those] killed and injured in motoring accidents has not fallen does not establish the lack of deterrence in the face of the increase in the potential population of drunken drivers."[6] The hard-line reforms may indeed be having a measureable impact on drunk driving incidents, death, and injuries—which is not readily apparent because other factors are concealing or masking their deterrent effect, such as changes in driving levels, vehicle mix, highway congestion, and alcoholic consumption.[7] It is encouraging that between 1977 and 1985 the rates of general alcohol-related fatalities decreased 22 percent per 100 million vehicle miles traveled and by 14 percent per 100,000 licensed drivers.[8]

DETERRENCE AND HIGH-RISK GROUPS

Repeaters and Specific Deterrence

Three groups that figure prominently in the drunk driving picture make achieving deterrence a formidable task: adolescent/young drivers, problem drivers/alcoholics, and recidivists. Specific deterrence refers to what effect the imposition of penalties (the severity of punishment) has on the subsequent drinking-driving behavior of those particular (specific) individuals. In this connection, we have already reviewed the limited impact that mandatory jail terms have had on deterring repeat offenders, that is, the effect of "specific" deterrence. Despite the tougher penalties and beefed-up rehabilitation programs, the recidivism rate is about 30 percent nationwide and over 50 percent in some places.[9]

Young Drivers

Various indices suggest that young drivers are at high risk for impaired-driving accidents. Each year, over 8,000 people between sixteen and twenty-four years old lose their lives in alcohol-related crashes, and an additional 50,000 suffer debilitating nonfatal injuries.[10] Drunk driving is the leading cause of death among teens, an estimated 85,000 of whom (fifteen to nineteen years) are injured in alcohol-related accidents annually.[11] Young adults eighteen to twenty-four years of age are disproportionately involved in alcohol-related traffic accidents and have the highest rates of arrests (per 100,000 drivers) of any age group.[12] A 1981 survey revealed that 41 percent of high school seniors admitted to "binge" drinking, that is, having five or more drinks on a single occasion within the past fourteen days.[13] The National Youth Study found that, in 1983, 42 percent of eighteen to twenty-four year-olds admitted to driving while intoxicated at least once during the last year.[14]

One of the most controversial attempts to control impaired driving among adolescents and youth was raising the minimum drinking age to twenty-one (see Close-up 13.1). At Yale University, students over twenty-one are served alcohol at social functions only if they present proper identification verifying age. "Dry" schools like the University of Missouri at Columbia take a totally different tack by banning all alcoholic beverages to the entire student body, thereby avoiding third-party liability suits at the same time. Once a favored drinking hangout for college students from nearby University of Texas, Sixth Street in Austin became a ghost town on weeknights since Texas raised the drinking age to twenty-one in September 1986.[15] Under Wisconsin's "not a drop" law, teenagers stopped by police who are found to have *any* detectable amount of alcohol in the blood routinely have their licenses suspended, a step that Connecticut and Maine have taken for youths with a .02 BAC or more.[16] At least twelve states impose a curfew on teenage drivers.[17]

SADD

The implicit philosophy behind designated-driver programs, Safe Rides, and Students Against Drunk Driving (SADD) is that many young people will simply refuse to say no to drinking in social situations and will be able to obtain alcoholic beverages despite the minimum drinking age, but they will say no to drinking and driving. Founded in 1981, SADD now has 15,000 chapters with about 4 million members. SADD began as a high school project in suburban Wayland (Massachusetts) when 900 students signed SADD "contracts" with their parents: they promised to call their parents whenever they have too much to drink or no designated-driver is available to take them home. In return, the parents agree to pick them up at any hour or place without asking any questions or reprimanding them at that time.[18]

Social Drinkers versus Problem Drinkers

Question:[19] "Is it reasonable to assume that those who are drunk or drugged at private parties or public drinking places, lacking the judgment and reflexes to drive safely, will calculate the increased penalties and choose not to drive?" Answer: "No, but they can decide not to drive to the event while they're still sober."[20]

The experts themselves are in sharp disagreement over how much of the DUI population is composed of problem drinkers or alcoholics v. social drinkers, and the relevance of deterrence for the former groups.[21] Some researchers maintain that "alcoholics and problem drinkers are at the heart of the problem of alcohol-involved accidents"—by some estimates 50 to 80 percent of all DUIs fall into this category—and believe that these heavy drinkers are not deterred by jail or other punitive countermeasures that might work for social drinkers.[22] "It may be possible to gain some marginal control of drinking before driving for light [social or casual] drinkers but not for heavy drinkers. Since the crash risk of light drinkers is minimal, the public health gains from deterring this group is negligible."[23]

It is probably true that persons who drink to .15 BAC or above are problem drinkers or alcoholics, and the drunk driver who kills is typically not the social drinker who simply has had one too many for the road: the NHTSA reports that the average BAC of a drinking driver killed in an accident is .20, twice the level of legal intoxication in almost every state.[24] On the other hand, there are authorities who contend that "certainly some DUI offenders are alcoholics, but not all or most," that DWI offenders are "midway between social drinkers and problem drinkers in drinking behavior," and that various studies point to the conclusion that DUI offenders and chronic alcohol abusers "cannot simply be equated."[25] Even the critics of deterrence acknowledge that "at least some heavy drinkers are capable of exercising restraint when cast in the driving role" either by cutting down on the amount of drinking before driving or by utilizing a designated-driver after a period of heavy drinking—the same position taken by the founder of MADD in response to the question posed at the introduction to this section.[26]

Close-up 13.1: Making 21 The National Minimum Drinking Age

From the time that Prohibition was repealed and states were given the right to regulate the liquor trade as they saw fit up until the early 1970s, the minimum drinking age in most states was 21.[a] This policy changed when the 26th Amendment to the Constitution, ratified in 1971, gave eighteen-year-olds the right to vote. Subsequently, during the 1970s many states lowered their legal drink age to eighteen in response to pressure from young persons who argued that if they were old enough to vote and go to war, they were old enough to drink.[b] Such action was taken in apparent disregard for its deleterious consequences and despite the fact that eighteen- to-twenty-year-olds are involved in 16 to 21 percent of all alcohol-related fatalities, yet make up only 10 percent of the licensed drivers and account for just 7 percent of total miles driven. In fact, drunk driving is the leading cause of death among teens.[c] When Michigan dropped its drinking age to eighteen, there was a 17 percent increase in accidents involving alcohol by eighteen- to 20-year-old drivers.[d]

Spearheaded by strong lobbying efforts by MADD and RID, in 1984 Congress enacted a federal statute encouraging all states to pass their own laws making it illegal for persons under twenty-one to purchase or possess alcoholic beverages. Any state that did not raise the minimum drink age to twenty-one (hereafter "21-M.D.A.") by October 1, 1986, risked losing their share of $10.6 billion in federal highway construction funds.[e] At the time the national minimum drinking age act was passed, twenty-eight states had a legal drinking age under twenty-one.[f] Under the threat of losing coveted transportation funds, one state after another raised their M.D.A. to twenty-one so that by the time of the federal deadline all but seven states were in compliance with the act; and by 1987 Wyoming and South Dakota were the only holdout states, but not for long.[g] After the Supreme Court removed any doubt about the validity of the 1984 federal statute,[h] Wyoming became the last state in the nation to adopt grudgingly a 21-M.D.A. law.[i] (Wyoming was losing $8-10 million a year in federal largesse and gaining the unsavory reputation as a "blood border" state because teenagers from surrounding areas were going there to drink and then driving home drunk late at night.)

Minimum drinking age laws tend to reduce the risk of an alcohol-related accident, but the overall amount of the reduction is difficult to gauge.[j] And, "as soon as one study is published showing a positive effect, another study emerges refuting that study and all previous studies."[k] Nonetheless, raising the legal drinking age to twenty-one is generally credited with a 10 to 15 percent decline in drunk driving fatalities among the eighteen- to twenty-year-olds who lost their drinking privileges.[l] (It helped Tennessee cut the nighttime fatality rate for nineteen and twenty-year-old drivers by 38 percent.[m]) It is possible, of course, for teenagers to circumvent the 21-M.D.A. by purchasing alcohol at places that do not ask for identification, and even easier to get someone else to buy drinks for them: After Massachusetts raised its drinking age, the number of underage persons who used others to obtain alcohol doubled from 21 percent to 43 percent.[m].

[a]*Drunk Driving Laws & Enforcement: An Assessment of Effectiveness,* Washington, D.C.: American Bar Association, February 1986, p. 39.

[b]Lawrence A. Greenfeld, Drunk Driving, *Bureau of Justice Statistics Special Report,* February 1988, p. 3.

[c]*Sunday New York Times,* October 5, 1986, p. 5; *American Bar Association Journal,* November 1984, p. 35; *USA Today,* October 9, 1986, p. 10A.

[d]Bruce Joel Hillman, "No More For The Road," *Kiwanis Magazine,* August 1986, p. 23.

[e]*ABA Journal,* November 1984, p. 35; 98 Stat.435,P.L.98-363

[f]Ibid.; *USA Today,* October 9, 1986, p. 10A.

[g]*USA Today,* Ibid., *New York Times,* December 21, 1987, p. B15.

[h]The suit brought by South Dakota claimed that the law was an impermissible infringment on "states rights." But the Court, refusing to address that issue, upheld the statute pursuant to the federal government's right to attach conditions to the receipt of federal funds.

[i] *New York Times,* July 1, 1988, p. A8; *South Dakota* v. *Dole,* Secretary of Transportation, No. 86-260. Decided June 23, 1987.

[j]*Drunk Driving Laws & Enforcement,* p. 39; Ralph Hingson et al., "Legal Interventions to Reduce Drunken Driving and Related Fatalities Among Youthful Drivers," *Alcohol, Drugs and Driving,* V 4, N 2, 1988, p. 97.

[k]*Drunk Driving Laws,* p. 39.

[l]Hingson, "Legal Interventions," p. 87; Ray McAllister, "The Drunken Driving Crackdown: Is It Working?" *ABA Journal,* September 1, 1988, p. 55; *USA Today,* October 1, 1986, p. 3A.

[m]*USA Today,* December 29, 1988, p. 6A.

[n]Hingson, "Legal Interventions," p. 93.

DETERMINANTS OF DRUNK DRIVING DETERRENCE

With few exceptions, the research on drunk driving deterrence shows that any gains derived from the new laws are short lived and that, as media attention subsides, within a year or so DUI behavior return to its previous levels.[27] This consistent finding is why people like Ross take a dim view of the "legal approach" in combating drunk driving: "Deterrence-based policies are questionable in the long run. No such policies have been scientifically demonstrated to work over time under conditions achieved in any jurisdiction."[28] An oft-cited example illustrating this point is the British Road Safety Act of 1967, under which the police were allowed to stop motorists on "reasonable suspicion," authorized to make wide use of breathalyzer tests to detect intoxicated motorists, and instructed to make enhanced efforts at strict enforcement. The highly publicized "breathalyzer blitz" was initially correlated with a marked drop in the number of fatal crashes involving alcohol, but after twelve months its deterrent impact had all but disappeared.[29]

Certainty of Apprehension

The two main determinants of deterring drunk driving are the chances of being caught (certainty of apprehension) and the severity of punishment if convicted. Deterrence is difficult to achieve because the certainty (likelihood) of detection is so low or uncertain: "On any given outing, an intoxicated driver has less than a 1-in-1,000 chance of being apprehended by the police."[30] Studies criticized for producing only short-term benefits document substantial deterrence so long as police enforcement levels of the new control measures remain high, that is, while conditions exist that increase the real and perceived risk of apprehension (see Close-up 13.2).[31] Maintaining deterrence is problematic, however, because over time, enforcement efforts invariably wane or become half-hearted and, "predictably, illusory threats do not long prove effective."[32] As the heightened enforcement effort lags, drivers soon come to realize that their actual likelihood of apprehension remains very low and drinking-driving behavior returns to "normal" levels.[33] For example, Maine's 1981 per se DUI law had an immediate one-year effect of reducing fatal crashes by 33 percent more than in control states. But by the end of the third year—when most citizens still thought it very unlikely drunk drivers would be stopped by the police—the rates had returned to the pre-law level.[34]

The continued minuscule likelihood of being caught DWI (see Figure 13.1) may explain why mandatory sentences are not more effective: why should DWI offenders be concerned about facing severe penalties upon conviction, since it will probably never come to that because their chances of being caught in the first place are so small? "Merely stiffening penalties, without a corresponding emphasis on apprehension by the police, will do little to get drunk

Figure 13.1
Number of Arrests for DUI per 100,000 Licensed Drivers, 1970-86

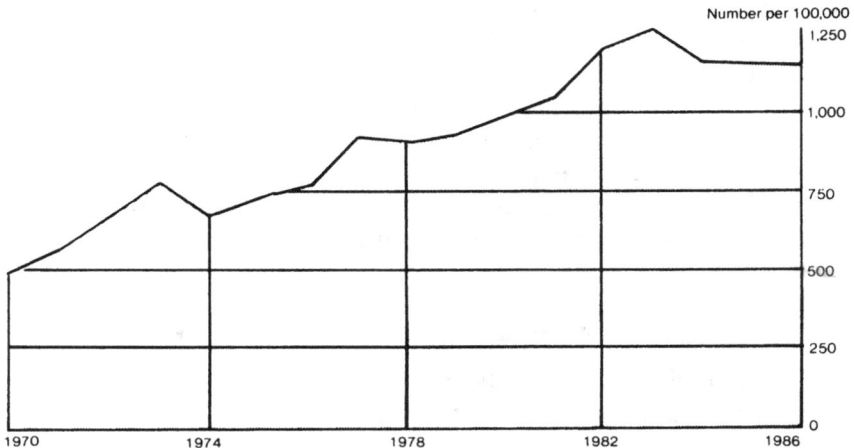

Although drunk drivers have an estimated 1 in 200 to 1 in 2,000 chance of being apprehended, the rate of arrest for DUI per 100,000 licensed drivers rose over 127 percent between 1970 and 1986. In the peak year, 1983, almost 2 million DUI arrests were made—about one arrest for every eighty licensed drivers in the nation. *Source:* Lawrence A. Greenfeld, Drunk Driving, *Bureau of Justice Statistics Special Report,* February 1988, p. 2.

drivers permanently off the road."[35] Viewed in this context, England's breathalyzer blitz "demonstrates important deterrent results for increased enforcement."[36] A longitudinal study of college students found that having been stopped by police while driving intoxicated "strongly predicted subsequent drunk driving" by virtue of altering the perception of the certainty of apprehension.[37]

Close up 13.2: Preventing Accidents through Concentrated Enforcement (PACE)*

Starting in 1980, for five months the Superior (Wisconsin) Police Department implemented a saturated enforcement program in a fifteen-square-block area of the city with the highest frequency of alcohol-related accidents on the weekends. The goal of project PACE was to increase substantially the number of arrests in the designated area, that is, to improve the certainty of apprehension.

This was accomplished by assigning three special PACE units to the high-accident beats; their only purpose was to screen major and minor traffic offenders for intoxicated drivers by making routine traffic arrests for moving and equipment violations. Extensive front-page newspaper and TV coverage of the project and issuing a large number of warning-citations were also used to reinforce public perception of the new strict enforcement policy. "As expected, the accident rate declined most during the Saturday period in which the PACE program was in effect for the most accident-prone times of the day. The accident frequency decreased from the 1979 figure of 44 to 26, a 31 percent decrease, and provided evidence of the magnitude of the PACE deterrent effect." And there was strong evidence that the stepped-up localized enforcement effort" impacted areas beyond the geographical bounderies of the PACE efforts" by reducing property damage and personal-injury accidents in contiguous sections of the city.

*Source: Gary W. Sykes, "Saturated Enforcement: The Efficacy of Deterrence Drunk Driving," *Journal of Criminal Justice* 12, no. 2 (1984), pp. 185-197.

Moral Component of Law versus Fear of Punishment

For the promotion of long-term control of drunk driving, Andeneas believes that the "moral component" of the laws are much more important than their direct legal threat of apprehension and punishment, that is, than the fear aspect of the laws. "From the legislator's perspective, creating moral inhibitions is of greater value than mere deterrence, because the former may work even when a person need not fear detection and punishment."[38] According to this view, the get-tough laws have a moral dimension that, through a very gradual and subtle process, fosters the development of personal attitudes that are intolerant of drinking-driving, and increase the number of role models and peer group members who eschew drinking-driving regardless of the perceived legal risks involved.[39] If this is true, then "the lack of discernible effects of the law on traffic deaths therefore neither proves nor disproves anything."[40] There is some evidence to support the operation of this morality factor in changing individual values and social norms, independent of the fear of punishment. "A small proportion of American drivers are exercising a degree of control over drinking or driving behavior despite a trivial risk of apprehension."[41] And some studies have found that higher levels of drunk driving are closely associated with the attitude that such behavior is *not* morally wrong and with having friends who do *not* disapprove of driving after drinking.[42] Conversely, "moral agreement" with drunk driving laws had a strong influence on inhibiting drinking and driving.[43]

Notes

CHAPTER 1

1. *USA Today,* March 30, 1989, p. 6A.
2. *Surgeon General's Workshop on Drunk Driving: Proceedings* (full report), Washington, D.C., December 14-16, 1988, p. 14.
3. One kind of alcoholic beverage affects the body and driving performance much like any other. A bottle of beer, for example, has the same amount of alcohol as a glass of wine or a shot of whiskey.
4. Lonn Lanza-Kaduce and Donna M. Bishop, "Legal Fictions and Criminology: The Jurisprudence of Drunk Driving," *Journal of Criminal Law and Criminology* 77, no. 2 (Summer 1986): 368; Statement by C. Everett Koop, *Surgeon General's Workshop on Drunk Driving: Proceedings, Press Conference,* Washington, D.C., May 31, 1989, p. 3; Bruce Joel Hillman, "No More For the Road," *Kiwanis* (August 1986): p. 22.
5. Hillman, "No More," p. 25; *Drunk Driving Laws and Enforcement: An Assessment of Effectiveness,* Washington, D.C.: American Bar Association, Criminal Justice Section, February 1986, p. 23; *The Drunk Driver May Kill You,* Allstate pamphlet, L746-8, p. 4.
6. Hillman, "No More," p. 23.
7. *Zeroing in on Repeat DWI Offenders, Conference on Recidivism: A Summary of the Proceedings,* National Commission Against Drunk Driving, Atlanta, Georgia, September 16, 1986, p. 45.
8. Hillman, "No More," p. 25.

9. *Zeroing in on Repeat DWI Offenders,* p. 45.

10. *USA Today,* April 7, 1989, p. 10A.

11. Hillman, "No More," p. 25.

12. *USA Today,* March 30, 1989, p. 6A.

13. *Drunk Driving Laws and Enforcement,* p. 23; Frank P. Williams and E. Lynn White, "What works? Legislative Actions Against Drunken Driving," *Research Bulletin,* Criminal Justice Center, Sam Houston University, no. 2 (1985): 4; *USA Today,* May 26, 1988, p. 14A.

14. *USA Today,* April 7, 1989, p. 10A.

15. *National Law Journal,* February 9, 1987, p. 8; *Newsweek,* September 13, 1982, p. 36.

16. *New York Times,* April 23, 1989, p. 25; Commercial Motor Vehicle Safety Act of 1986, Title XII of the Anti-Drug Abuse Act of 1986.

17. Thomas J. Hammer, "Offense Definition in Wisconsin's Impaired Driving Statutes," *Marquette Law Review* 69, no. 2 (Winter 1986): 196-197.

18. Ralph Hingson et al., "Legal Interventions to Reduce Drunken Driving and Related Fatalities Among Youthful Drivers," *Alcohol, Drugs and Driving* 4, no. 2, p. 88.

19. Williams and White, "What Works?" p. 1; *USA Today,* December 9, 1987, p. 9A; *USA Today,* February 29, 1988, p. 1.

20. Hillman, "No More," p. 23; Lance J. Rogers, "The Drunk-Driving Roadblock: Random Seizure or Minimal Intrusion?" *Criminal Law Bulletin* (May-June 1985): 201.

21. *Fatal Accident Reporting System (FARS), 1987,* National Highway Safety Administration, December 1988, n.p.; *Crime Control Digest,* December 26, 1988, p. 9.

22. *Jailing Drunk Drivers: Impact on the Criminal Justice System,* NIJ Research in Brief, November 1984, n.p.

23. *Newsweek,* September 13, 1982, p. 34.

24. Frank P. Williams and E. Lynn White, "Legislative Actions Against Drunken Driving: An Assessment with Additional Evidence on the Open Container," *Criminal Justice Policy Review* 1, no. 3 (10/86): 287.

25. Ray R. Lewis and Lawrence W. Sherman, *Drunk Driving Tests in Fatal Accidents,* Crime Control Reports #3, Crime Control Institute, Washington, D.C., December 1986, p. 6.

26. *Alcohol Involvement in Fatal Traffic Crashes (1988),* National Highway Traffic Safety Administration, July 1989, p. 5; *Traffic Fatality Facts, 1988* (twelve-page fact sheet), National Highway Safety Administration, July 1989, p. 2.

27. James B. Jacobs, *Drinking and Crime,* National Institute of Justice, Crime File Study Guide, n.d., n.p.; *Traffic Fatality Facts,* p. 2; *Alcohol Involvement in Fatal Traffic Crashes* (1988), p. 5.

28. *ABA Journal* (September 1983): 1202; *USA Today,* December 29, 1988, p. 6A; Hillman, "No More," p. 23; *Drunk Driver and Jail,* vol. 1, National Highway Traffic Safety Administration, January 1986.

29. *Newsweek,* September 13, 1982, p. 34; Hillman, "No More," p. 23.

30. *USA Today,* December 29, 1988, p. 6A; James R. Acker, "Social Sciences and the Criminal Law: A Report on America's War Against Drunk Driving," *Criminal Law Bulletin* (July-August 1989): 382.

CHAPTER 2

1. Daniel W. Moylan, "New Approach to an Old Problem," *ABA Journal* (January 1983): 46.

2. Bruce Joel Hillman, "No More For The Road," *Kiwanis* (August 1986): 23.

3. *Newsweek,* September 13, 1982, p. 35.

4. *Hartford Courant,* September 25, 1988, p. C3.

5. Williams and White, "What Works?" p. 2.

6. Hillman, "No More," p. 23.

7. Lynn S. Adelman, introduction to special issue on DWI, *Marquette Law Review* 69, no. 2 (Winter 1986): 159.

8. *Presidential Commission on Drunk Driving, Final Report,* November 1982, p. 2.

9. Ray McAllister, "The Drunken Driving Crackdown: Is It Working?" *ABA Journal* (September 1, 1988): 55; *USA Today,* December 21, 1987, p. 1.

10. McAllister, "The Drunken Driving Crackdown," p. 55.

11. *Changes in Alcohol-Involved Fatal Crashes Associated with Tougher State Alcohol Legislation,* report by Sigmastat Inc., Brookeville, Md., July 1989, pp. 1-2.

12. Ralph Hingson et al., "Legal Interventions to Reduce Drunken Driving and Related Fatalities Among Youthful Drivers," *Alcohol, Drugs and Driving* 4, no. 2, p. 89; Richard A. Ball and J. Robert Lilly, "The Potential Use of Home Incarceration for Drunken Drivers," *Crime & Delinquency* (April 1986): 231.

13. *ABA Journal* (September 1983): 1203.

14. *Zeroing in on Repeat DWI Offenders,* inside cover and communications with National Commission.

15. Pamphlet from National Commission Against Drunk Driving, especially their 1988 Executive Summary.

16. *Surgeon General's Workshop on Drunk Driving: Proceedings,* Rockville, Md.: U.S. Department of Health and Human Services, 1989.

17. These warnings are required on alcoholic beverage containers as of November 1989.

18. *Banning Alcohol Advertising,* transcript, Oprah Winfrey Show, July 19, 1989.

19. Oprah Winfrey transcript.

20. *American Bar Association Journal* (September 1983): 1202.

CHAPTER 3

1. John Gales Sauls, "Traffic Stops: Police Powers Under the Fourth Amendment," *FBI Law Enforcement Bulletin* (September 1989): p. 28.

2. Yale Kamisar, Wayne LaFave, and Jerold Israel, *Modern Criminal Procedure,* St. Paul, Minn.: West Publishing, 1980, p. 268.

3. Thomas Gardner and Victor Manian, *Principles and Cases of the Law of Arrest, Search and Seizure,* New York: McGraw-Hill, 1974, pp. 14-18; J. Shane Creamer, *The Law of Arrest, Search, and Seizure,* Philadelphia: W. B. Saunders, 1968, p. 11.

4. The officer may order the driver to exit the car as a matter of ensuring police safety but obviously cannot force the subject to perform any field tests.

5. Sauls, September 1989, p. 29.

6. *Standardized Field Sobriety Testing,* International Association of Chiefs of Police, Training Key No. 365, 1987, five pages; Evelyn Vingilis and Violet Vingilis, "The Importance of Roadside Screening for Impaired Drivers in Canada," *Canadian Journal of Criminology* 29, no. 1 (January 1987): 25.

7. *New York Times,* January 18, 1987, p. 34; *ABA Journal* (May 1985): 28.

8. It can also be conducted without having the driver leave the car, although this is not the preferred procedure.

9. *New York Times,* January 3, 1988, p. 20; Northwestern University tape; Training Key 365, IACP.

10. *New York Times,* January 3, 1988, p. 20.

11. Training Key 365, 25.

12. *State v Superior Court (Blake),* 149 Ariz. 269, 718 P.2d 171, 60 ALR4th 1103 (1986); Robert H. Reeder, "Legal Aspects of Horizontal Gaze Nystagmus," publication of Northwestern University Traffic Institute.

CHAPTER 4

1. Donald H. Nichols, ed., *Drinking/Driving Law Letter,* Wilmette, Ill.: Callaghan, 1986.

2. *U.S.* v. *Brignoni-Ponce,* 422 U.S. 873 (1975).

3. *Delaware* v. *Prouse,* No. 77-1571, Decided March 27, 1979.

4. Lance J. Rogers, "The Drunk-Driving Roadblock: Random Seizure or Minimal Intrusion?" *Criminal Law Bulletin* (May-June 1985): pp. 197-198.

5. *Ibid.,* p. 202.

6. *Crime Control Digest* (August 25, 1986): 7; *Nelson* v. *Lane County,* S33066.

7. Fred Leeson, "Ore. Court Strikes Down Sobriety Checkpoints," *National Law Journal* (October 12, 1987): 9.

8. *New York Times,* December 27, 1987, E4; Leeson, "Ore. Court Strikes Down," p. 9.

9. *Drunk Driving Laws and Enforcement: An Assessment of Effectiveness,* Washington, D.C.: American Bar Association, Criminal Justice Section, February 1986, p. 28.

10. Gail Diane Cox, "Calif. Court Oks Administrative Roadblocks," *National Law Journal,* November 23, 1987, p. 8.

11. *Drunk Driving Laws and Enforcement,* p. 28.

12. *U.S. Law Week,* April 22, 1986, p. 2522.

13. Jerome O. Campane, "The Constitutionality of Drunk Driver Roadblocks," *FBI Law Enforcement Bulletin* (July 1984): 28.

14. Rogers, "The Drunk Driving Roadblock," p. 211.

15. *Drunk Driving Laws and Enforcement,* p. 4.

16. *54 Law Week* 2155, September 24, 1985.

17. *New York Times,* November 2, 1987, p. D15; *Drunk Driving Laws and Enforcement,* pp. 22-23.

18. *ABA Journal,* January 1, 1986, p. 126; Rogers, "The Drunk Driving Roadblock," pp. 213-214; *ABA Journal,* January 1, 1986, p. 126; *State* v. *Koppel,* No. 85-006, August 16, 1985.

19. *USA Today,* August 18, 1987, p. 9A.

20. Rogers, "The Drunk Driving Roadblock," pp. 213-214.

21. *Crime Control Digest,* August 25, 1986, p. 7.

22. Rogers, "The Drunk Driving Roadblock," pp. 214-215.

23. *Michigan Department of State Police* v. *Sitz,* 110 S.Ct. 2481 (1990).

CHAPTER 5

1. Evelyn Vingilis and Violet Vingilis, "The Importance of Roadside Screening for Impaired Drivers in Canada," *Canadian Journal of Criminology* 29, no. 1 (January 1987): 25.

2. Donald Nichols, ed., *Drinking/Driving Law Letter,* Willmette, Ill.: Callaghan, 1986, chap. 26, p. 20.

3. *Drunk Driving Laws and Enforcement,* Washington, D.C.: American Bar Assocation, February 1986, p. 47; *Presidential Commission on Drunk Driving, Final Report,* p. 15.

4. *Presidential Commission, ibid.,* p. 15.

5. *IACP News,* July 1989, n.p.

6. *Changes in Alcohol-Involved Fatal Crashes Associated with Tougher State Alcohol Legislation,* report by Sigmastat Inc., Brookesville, Md., July 1989, p. 24.

7. *Drunk Driving Laws and Enforcement,* pp. 47, 57-59; Vingilis and Vingilis, pp. 26-28.

8. Nichols, *Drinking/Driving Law Letter,* chap. 26, pp. 23-24.

9. *Drunk Driving Laws and Enforcement,* p. 57.

10. *New York Times,* August 20, 1985, p. A14.

11. *Ibid.*

12. *Newsweek* (International Edition), October 7, 1985, p. 3; Nichols, *Law Letter,* chap. 26, p. 24.

CHAPTER 6

1. *Presidential Commission, Final Report,* p. 18.

2. *Newsweek,* September 13, 1982, p. 39.

3. *Network Newsnotes,* National Commission Against Drunk Driving (Summer 1989): p. 7.

4. *Drunk Driving Laws and Enforcement,* Washington, D.C.: American Bar Association, February 1986, p. 80.

5. *Zeroing in on Repeat DWI Offenders, Conference on Recidivism: A Summary of the Proceedings,* National Commission Against Drunk Driving, Atlanta, Georgia, September 16, 1986, p. 17.

6. *Ibid.; Presidential Commission, Final Report,* p. 20; *Drunk Driving Laws and Enforcement,* pp. 65-66.

7. *ABA Journal,* January 1985, p. 135.

8. *Drunk Driving Laws and Enforcement,* p. 79.

9. *Mackey* v. *Montrym,* 99 S.Ct. 2612, 1979.

10. *Network Newsnotes* (Summer 1987): 7.

11. *Presidential Commission,* p. 20.

12. *Zeroing in on,* p. 17.

13. *Network Newsnotes* (Summer 1989): 7.

14. *Ibid.; Surgeon General's Workshop on Drunk Driving* (full report) pp. 47-48.

15. Hans C. Joksch, *The Impact of Severe Penalties on Drinking and Driving,* Washington, D.C.: AAA Foundation for Traffic Safety, May 1988, p. 5; *Surgeon General's Workshop* (full report) p. 47.

16. *Presidential Commission* (full report), p. 21.

17. James R. Acker, "Social Sciences and the Criminal Law: a Report on America's War against Drunk Driving," *Criminal Law Bulletin* (July-August 1989): 387; *ABA Journal* (December 1982): 1551-1554.

18. *Newsweek,* September 13, 1982, p. 39.

19. *Surgeon General's Workshop on Drunk Driving: Proceedings,* Washington, D.C., December 14-16, 1988, p. 5.

20. *Network Newsnotes* (Summer 1989): p. 7.

21. Robert B. Voas, "Evaluation of Jail as a Penalty for Drunk Driving," *Alcohol, Drugs and Driving* 2, no. 2 (1986): 65.

22. *Changes in Alcohol-Involved Fatal Crashes Associated With Tougher State Alcohol Legislation,* report by Sigmastat Inc., Brookesville, Md., July 1989, pp. 25-26; Robert B. Voas, "Evaluation of Jail as a Penalty for Drunk Driving," *Alcohol, Drugs and Driving* 2, no. 2 (1986): 64.

23. Ray McAllister, "The Drunken Driving Crackdown: Is It Working?" *ABA Journal* (September 1, 1988): 55.

24. *Network Newsnotes* (Summer 1989): 7.

25. *Ibid., Network Newsnotes,* 6-7.

26. *Sigmastat Inc. report,* p. 18.

27. *Network Newsnotes* (Summer 1987): 7; *Newsweek,* December 21, 1987, pp. 42-43.

28. *The Drunk Driver and Jail: Alternatives to Jail,* National Highway Traffic Safety Administration, U.S. Dept. of Transportation 2 (January 1986): viii.

CHAPTER 7

1. *Pennsylvania* v. *Bruder* 109 S.Ct. 205, 1988; *Berkemer* v. *McCarty* 468 U.S. 420, 1984.

2. *South Dakota* v. *Neville,* 103 S.Ct. 916, 1983.

3. Robert J. Craddick, "Blood-Alcohol Tests: Neville and its Progeny," *Criminal Law Bulletin* (November-December 1984): 505.

4. By silence, shaking head "no," or explicit statements of refusal.

5. Craddick, "Blood-Alcohol Tests," p. 513.

6. *Ibid.,* pp. 512-514.

7. *ABA Journal* (January 1985): 135.

8. Laurie A. Mlsna, "Public Outcry v. Individual Rights: Right to Counsel and the Drunk Driver's Dilemma," *Marquette Law Review* 69, no. 2 (Winter 1986): 296.

9. *California* v. *Trombetta,* 52 U.S.L.W. 4747 (1984).

10. In *Blanton* v. *North Las Vegas* (1989), the Supreme Court declared that persons charged with DUI do not have a constitutional right to a jury trial if the offense carries a jail sentence of six months or less. The Court based its decision on a long-held distinction between petty offenses and serious offenses, as defined by the maximum period of incarceration. Nevada is one of five states that do not allow jury trials for DUI defendants.

11. *New York Times,* March 23, 1987, p. A15.

12. *New York Times,* November 3, 1985, p. 8.

13. Lloyd Kilpack, "Use of a Video Camera for DUI Investigations," *FBI Law Enforcement Bulletin* (May 1987): 7-9.

14. *Drunk Driving Laws and Enforcement,* p. 49.

15. *Insight,* May 25, 1987, p. 49.

16. *Youth Driving Without Impairment: Report on the Youth Impaired Driving Public Hearings,* prepared by National Commission Against Drunk Driving, Washington, D.C., n.d., p. 31.

17. *Network Newsnotes* (Spring 1989), with update data supplied to author by *Network News.*

18. *New York Times,* December 13, 1987, p. 73.

19. Donald H. Nichols, *Drinking/Driving Litigation: Criminal and Civil,* Wilmette, Ill.: Callaghan, 1987, chap. 28, p. 1; Joseph W. Little, "Drinking, Driving and the Law," *Criminal Justice Abstracts* (June 1980): 264.

20. *ABA Journal* (September 1983): 1202.

21. Donald H. Nichols, ed., *Drinking/Driving Law Letter,* Wilmette, Ill.: Callaghan, 1986, chap. 28, pp. 2-3.

22. Donald H. Nichols, "Toward A Coordinated Judicial View of the Accuracy of Breath Testing Devices," *North Dakota Law Review* 59, no. 3 (1983): 329-348.

23. California v. Trombetta 104 S.Ct. 2528, 1984.

24. John Albrecht, *Processing Charges of Driving Under the Influence of Alcohol/Drugs in Montana,* agency report, Montana Highway Safety Traffic Division.

25. Evelyn Vingilis and Violet Vingilis, "The Importance of Roadside Screening for Impaired Drivers in Canada," *Canadian Journal of Criminology* 29, no. 1 (January 1987): 27.

26. *USA Today,* August 18, 1987, p. 9A.

27. *Drunk Driving Laws and Enforcement,* p. 32

28. *Newsweek,* September 13, 1982, p. 35.

29. *New York Times,* January 18, 1987, p. 34.

30. *Ibid.*

31. *Jailing Drunk Drivers: Impact on the Criminal Justice System,* NIJ Research in Brief, November 1984.

32. Drunk Driving Laws and Enforcement, p. 32.

CHAPTER 8

1. *Time,* January 16, 1984, p. 62.

2. *National Law Journal,* October 12, 1987, p. 51.

3. *New York Times,* August 28, 1989, pp. B1 and B4.

4. Challenging the legality of the initial stop and subsequent arrest is another line of defense used.

5. *Drunk Driving Laws and Enforcement,* Washington, D.C.: American Bar Association, February 1986, p. 32.

6. *National Law Journal,* February 9, 1987, p. 8.

7. *Insight,* November 7, 1988, p. 52; *Crime Control Digest,* November 21, 1988, p. 6.

8. *New York Times,* August 28, 1989, p. B1.

9. *Inside Edition,* November 8, 1989.

10. Andrew Blum, "New Drunken-Driving Defense Causes a Stir," *National Law Journal,* April 18, 1988, p. 7.

11. This is an advantage of on-site BATmobile testing.

12. *Laws and Enforcement,* p. 33.

13. James R. Acker, "Social Sciences and the Criminal Law," *Criminal Law Bulletin* (July-August 1989): 386.

14. *Drunk Driving and Alcohol Law Report,* undated brochure; Michele Galen, "Key-Drunken Defense Shot Down in N.J.," *National Law Journal,* July 27, 1987, p. 27.

15. *Time,* January 16, 1984, p. 62.

16. Donald Nichols, *ABA Journal,* May 1985, p. 28.

17. *Ibid.*

18. *Time,* January 16, 1984, p. 62.

19. *Newsweek,* September 13, 1982, pp. 34-39.

CHAPTER 9

1. *Jailing Drunk Drivers: Impact on the Criminal Justice System,* NIJ Research in Brief, November 1984; Robert B. Voas, "Evaluation of Jail as a Penalty for Drunk Driving," *Alcohol, Drugs and Driving* 2, no. 2 (1986): p. 47; John R. Snortum et al., "Deterring Alcohol-Impaired Driving," *Justice Quarterly* (June 1986): 140.

2. *Ibid.*

3. Examples include New Jersey, New Mexico, California, Colorado, Ohio, and Tennessee.

4. *Drunk Driving Laws and Enforcement,* Washington, D.C.: American Bar Association, February 1986, p. 81.

5. *Newsweek,* September 13, 1982, p. 35.

6. *Boston Globe,* February 16, 1987, p. 20.

7. Voas, "Evaluation," pp. 48, 53; *Time,* January 16, 1984, p. 62; *The Drunk Driver and Jail: Alternatives to Jail,* National Highway Traffic Safety Administration, U.S. Dept. of Transportation 2 (January 1986): vii.

8. Voas, "Evaluation," p. 53.

9. *Drunk and Deadly: A Day on America's Highways,* HBO Special, May 17, 1987.

10. *Laws and Enforcement,* p. 89.

11. H. Laurence Ross and James P. Foley, "Judicial Disobediance of the Mandate to Imprison Drunk Drivers," *Law & Society Review* 21, no. 2 (1987): 315-323.

12. Time spent in pretrial detention or incurred as part of the booking process.

13. *Ibid.,* pp. 318-319.

14. *Ibid.,* p. 316.

15. *Ibid.,* p. 318.

16. *Laws and Enforcement,* p. 95; Ross and Foley, "Judicial Disobediance," p. 318.

17. *Laws and Enforcement,* p. 95.

18. Ross and Foley, "Judicial Disobediance," p. 320.

19. Thomas A. Cowan, et al., "How Judges View Drunk Driving Laws: A Survey," *Judges Journal* 24, no. 4 (Fall 1985): 4ff.

20. *Zeroing in on Repeat DWI Offenders, Conference on Recidivism: A Summary of the Proceedings,* National Commission Against Drunk Driving, Atlanta, Georgia, September 16, 1986, p. 56.

21. Cowan, "How Judges," p. 54; *Zeroing in on,* p. 57.

22. Ross and Foley, "Judicial," p. 321.

23. *Ibid., p. 320.*

24. *Laws and Enforcement,* p. 95; Voas, "Evaluation," p. 61.

25. *Zeroing in on,* pp. 57, 65.

26. *Ibid.,* p. 57.

27. Voas, "Evaluation," p. 54.

28. Frank P. Williams and E. Lynn White, "What Works? Legislative Actions Against Drunken Driving," *Research Bulletin,* Criminal Justice Center, Sam Houston University, no. 2 (1985): 7.

29. McAllister, "The Drunken Driving Crackdown," p. 54.

30. Voas, "Evaluation," p. 56.

31. *Ibid.,* pp. 56-57.

32. *Ibid.,* p. 62; *Laws and Enforcement,* passim.

33. Voas, "Evaluation," p. 65.

34. *Ibid.,* p. 66; *Presidential Commission, Final Report,* p. 5.

35. Voas, "Evaluation," p. 65.

36. *Ibid.,* pp. 56-57; *Laws and Enforcement,* p. 89.

37. *Community Service as an Alternative Sentence for DUI Convictions,* prepared by Automotive Transportation Center, A.A. Potter Engineering Center, West Lafayette, Indiana, August 1987, p. 1.

38. *Jailing Drunk Drivers,* NIJ Research in Brief, and full report p. 21; *Laws and Enforcement,* p. 90.

39. *The Drunk Driver and Jail,* vol. 2, p. vii.

40. *Community Service as Alternative,* pp. 1, 15.

41. *The Drunk Driver and Jail,* vol. 2, p. vii; *Presidential Commission, Final Report,* p. 18.

42. *Community Service as Alternative,* p. 1.

43. *Drunk Driver and Jail,* vol. 2, p. 1.

44. *Ibid.,* p. vii.

45. *Ibid.,* p. vii.

46. Carmen A. Cicchetti and Louise A. Enos, *Driving Under the Influence of Liquor: An Analysis Four Years after Chapter 373,* Massachusetts Trial Court (Boston), June 12, 1987, pp. 17-19.

47. *Jailing Drunk Drivers,* full report, May 1985, pp. 32-33; *ABA Journal,* February 1982, p. 140; Joksch, "The Impact of," p. 5.

CHAPTER 10

1. *New York Times,* December 25, 1986, p. 15; *Time,* January 12, 1987, p. 35.

2. *Jailing Drunk Drivers: Impact on the Criminal Justice System* (executive summary), May 1985, pp. 17-34.

3. James Frank et al., "Police Attitudes Toward DUI Legislation," *Journal of Police Science and Administration* (December 1987): p. 311.

4. *Zeroing in on Repeat DWI Offenders, Conference on Recidivism: A Summary of the Proceedings,* National Commission Against Drunk Driving, Atlanta, Georgia, September 16, 1986, p. 56.

5. Robert B. Voas, "Evaluation of Jail as a Penalty for Drunk Driving," Alcohol, Drugs and Driving 2, no. 2 (1986) p. 61.

6. *Ibid.,* pp. 61-62.

7. *Ibid.*

8. Diversion to an alcohol education or treatment program.

9. *The Justice Analyst,* Pennsylvania Commission on Crime and Delinquency, Bureau of Statistics and Policy Research, October 1988, p. 3.

10. *Jailing Drunk Drivers,* full report, p. 28.

11. *New York Times,* August 13, 1989, p. 16; *New York Times,* December 29, 1987, p. 8.

12. Daniel P. LeClair (principal investigator), *The Use of Prison Confinement for the Treatment of Multiple Drunken Driver Offenders: A Process Evaluation of the Longwood Treatment Center* (executive summary), agency report, Massachusetts Department of Correction, June 1987, general reference.

13. *Ibid.,* p. 4.

14. *New York Times,* October 4, 1987, p. 10; *Hartford Courant,* May 7, 1990, p. 1ff.

15. *New York Times,* December 11, 1988, p. 18.

16. *Sunday New York Times,* August 13, 1989, p. 16.

17. Daniel W. Moyln, "New Approach to an Old Problem," *ABA Journal* (January 1983): 46-49.

CHAPTER 11

1. *New York Times,* December 24, 1988, p. 48.

2. *Washington Post* (Maryland Weekly), May 15, 1986, p. 1 ff; *New Haven Register,* November 8, 1987, p. A26.

3. *New Haven Register,* November 8, 1987, p. A26; *National Law Journal,* February 9, 1987, p. 8.

4. *USA Today,* December 29, 1988, p. 6A; *New York Times,* December 24, 1988, p. 48; Interlock package material from Donald W. Collier, *Guardian Technologies.*

5. *Crime Control Digest,* November 30, 1987, p. 2; *USA Today,* December 29, 1988, p. 6A.

6. *Washington Post,* May 15, 1986, p. 1ff.

7. *New York Times,* August 6, 1987, p. B1.

8. *New Haven Register,* November 8, 1987, p. A26.

9. *New York Times,* December 24, 1988, p. 48

10. *New York Times,* August 6, 1987, p. B1.

11. As often as every sixty days.

12. *Newsweek,* December 21, 1987, p. 42.

13. *Washington Post,* May 15, 1986, p. 1ff.

14. *Ibid.*; *New York Times,* December 24, 1988, p. 48.

15. *Newsweek,* December 21, 1987, p. 42.

16. *New York Times,* December 24, 1988, p. 48.

17. Interlock package, *Guardian Technologies.*

18. Ibid.

19. National Law Journal, February 9, 1987, p. 8.

20. Visitors are prepared for what they are about to see with a slide show of accidents and a talk on the consequences of drunk driving.

21. *Community Service as an Alternative Sentence for DUI Convictions,* report prepared by Automotive Transportation Center, A.A. Potter Engineering Center, West Lafayette, Indiana, August 1987, p. 7; *New York Times,* September 21, 1988, p. 10.

22. *New York Times,* September 21, 1988, p. 10.

23. Letter to author from Sacramento Superior Court Judge Jeffrey L. Gunther.

24. *Ibid.*

25. *ABA Journal,* January 1985, p. 36.

26. *National Law Journal,* June 6, 1988, p. 51.

27. *USA Today,* December 21, 1987, p. 1.

28. *Newsweek,* September 13, 1982, p. 37.

29. *Insight,* August 31, 1987, p. 53.

30. *New York Times,* July 30, 1987, p. A21.

31. *Newsweek,* February 23, 1976, p. 44.

CHAPTER 12

1. Unless otherwise indicated, *liability* always refers to suits against third parties, notably licensed servers or social hosts, rather than suits against the drunk drivers themselves or other third parties such as police officers.

2. Joseph W. Little, "Drinking, Driving and the Law," *Criminal Justice Abstracts* (June 1980): p. 277.

3. *ABA Journal,* September 1984, p. 31.

4. Carla K. Smith, "Social Host Liability for Injuries Caused by the Acts of an Intoxicated Guest," *North Dakota Law Review* 59, no. 3 (1983): 449; Grant Pierson, "Server vs. Driver Liability: A Suggested Change to

Reduce Drinking and Driving," *Northern Illinois University Law Review* 7, no. 2 (Spring 1987): 265.

5. James M. Goldberg, "One for the Road," *ABA Journal,* June 1, 1987, pp. 84ff.

6. Pierson, "Server vs. Driver," p. 260.

7. *Ibid.,* pp. 261-262; Robert W. Gomulkiewicz, "Recognizing the Liability of Social Hosts Who Knowingly Allow Intoxicated Guests to Drive: Limits to Socially Acceptable Behavior," *Washington Law Review* 60, no. 2 (1985) p. 390.

8. Goldberg, "One for," p. 86.

9. *Ibid.; ABA Journal,* September 1984, p. 31.

10. *New York Times,* August 9, 1985, p. 1ff.

11. *National Law Journal,* March 23, 1987, p. 29.

12. *Buffalo News,* August 16, 1986, p. 5ff.

13. *New York Times,* August 9, 1985, p. 1ff.

14. *New York Times,* December 8, 1985, p. 64.

15. Goldberg, "One for," p. 88.

16. *Buffalo News,* August 16, 1986, p. 5ff.

17. *Newsweek,* September 13, 1982, p. 39.

18. *New York Times,* August 9, 1985, p. 1ff; Goldberg, "One for," p. 86; Little, "Drinking, Driving," p. 277.

19. *Training for Intervention by Servers of Alcohol Program.*

20. *Drunk Driving Laws and Enforcement: An Assessment of Effectiveness,* Washington, D.C.: American Bar Association, February 1986, p. 121.

21. *Ibid.,* pp. 121-122.

22. *Ibid.,* p. 113.

23. Goldberg, "One for," p. 88.

24. *New York Times,* October 31, 1988, p. A12.

25. Little, "Drinking, Driving," p. 277.

26. Derry D. Sparlin, "Social Host Liability for Guests Who Drink and Drive: A Closer Look at the Benefits and the Burdens," *William and Mary Law Review* 27, no. 3 (Spring 1986): 604; Smith, "Social Host Liability," pp. 447, 475; Pamela Lindmark, "View of Social-Host Liability Expanded in Mass.," *National Law Journal,* September 8, 1986, p. 5; Deborah Goldberg, "Imposition of Liability on Social Hosts in Drunk Driving Cases: A Judicial Response Mandated by Principles of Common Law and Common Sense," *Marquette Law Review* 69, no. 2 (Winter 1986): p. 252.

27. *ABA Journal,* July 1985, p. 94; *U.S. Law Week,* September 24, 1985, p. 1045; Gomulkiewicz, "Recognizing," p. 391; Goldberg, "Imposition," p. 254.

28. Smith, "Social Host Liability," pp. 459, 447; *Rappaport v. Nichols,* 31 N.J. 188, 156 A.2d 1 (1959); Pierson, "Server vs.," p. 264.

29. *ABA Journal,* October 1984, p. 182.

30. The decision did not apply to situations involving many guests, or to a host who is preoccupied with other matters and thereafter unable personally to serve alcohol to individual guests.

31. ABA Journal, October 1984, p. 182.

32. New York Times, June 20, 1986, p. B5; ABA Journal, October 1984, pp. 180ff.

33. Smith, "Social Host Liability," p. 464.

34. Sparlin, "Social Host Liability," p. 604; Smith, "Social Host Liability," pp. 462-464.

35. Goldberg, "Imposition of," p. 263.

36. Smith, "Social Host Liability," p. 475.

37. Goldberg, "One for," p. 88.

38. Sparlin, "Social Host," pp. 585, 608.

39. Goldberg, "Imposition," p. 257; Goldberg, "One for," p. 88.

40. Smith, "Social Host," p. 453; ABA Journal, September 1984, p. 31; Sparlin, "Social Host," pp. 607-608.

CHAPTER 13

1. Ray McAllister, "The Drunken Driving Crackdown: Is It Working? ABA Journal, September 1, 1988, p. 54; James R. Acker, "Social Sciences and the Criminal Law: A Report on America's War against Drunk Driving," Criminal Law Bulletin, July-August 1989, p. 381.

2. New York Times, October 29, 1987, p. A18.

3. New York Times, October 29, 1987, p. A18.

4. USA Today, December 29, 1988, p. 6A; New York Times, December 15, 1988, p. A34.

5. Hartford Courant, May 6, 1990, p. A16.

6. Harold L. Votey, "The Deterioration of Deterrence Effects of Drunk Driving Legislation," Journal of Criminal Justice 12, no. 2 (1984): p. 126.

7. Ibid., p. 127.

8. Dennis M. Donovan, "Driving While Intoxicated: Different Roads To and From the Problem," Criminal Justice and Behavior, September 1989, 272.

9. Interlock package, Guardian Technologies.

10. Bruce Joel Hillman, "No More for the Road," Kiwanis, August 1986, p. 23.

11. Statement by C. Everett Koop, Surgeon General's Workshop on Drunk Driving: Proceedings, Press Conference, Washington, D.C., May 31, 1989; ABA Journal, November 1984, p. 351.

12. Lonn Lanza-Kaduce, "Perceptual Deterrence and Drinking and Driving Among College Students," Criminology (May 1988): 321.

13. James B. Jacobs, Drinking and Crime, NIJ, Crime File Study Guide, no date.

14. Delbert Elliott, "Self-Reported Driving While Under the Influence of Alcohol/Drugs and the Risk of Alcohol/Drug-Related Accidents," *Alcohol, Drugs and Driving* 3, no. 3-4: 34.

15. *New York Times,* December 21, 1987, p. B15.

16. *New York Times,* March 23, 1987, p. A15; *New Haven Register,* April 26, 1990, p. 7; *Law Enforcement News,* March 29, 1988, p. 5.

17. *ABA Journal,* September 1983, pp. 1201-1204.

18. *Newsweek,* September 13, 1982, p. 39.

19. Asked of MADD founder at a conference for judges.

20. *Zeroing in,* p. 63.

21. The terms are used interchangeably in the literature and without precise definition.

22. *Zeroing in,* p. 63.

23. John R. Snortum et al., "Deterring Alcohol-Impaired Driving: A Comparative Analysis of Compliance in Norway and the United States," *Justice Quarterly* (June 1986): 161.

24. *Ibid.; Newsweek,* September 13, 1982, p. 35.

25. *Zeroing in,* pp. 2, 4.

26. Snortum, "Deterring," p. 161; John R. Snortum and Dale E. Berger, "Drinking and Driving: Detecting the 'Dark Figure' of Compliance," *Journal of Criminal Justice* 14, no. 6 (1986): p. 475.

27. Robert B. Voas, "Evaluation of Jail as a Penalty for Drunk Driving," *Alcohol, Drugs and Driving* 2, no. 2 (1986): 56; Williams and White, "Legislative Actions," *Criminal Justice Policy Review,* p. 288; Bonnie Steinbock, "Drunk Driving," *Philosophy and Public Affairs* 14, no. 3 (1985): p. 292.

28. Snortum, "Deterring," p. 142.

29. Joseph W. Little, "Drinking, Driving and the Law," *Criminal Justice Abstracts* (June 1980): 280; Gary W. Sykes, "Saturated Enforcement: The Efficacy of Deterrence and Drunk Driving," *Journal of Criminal Justice* 12, no. 2 (1984): 188.

30. Acker, "Social Sciences," p. 384; Dennis M. Donovan, "Driving While Intoxicated: Different Roads To and From the Problem," *Criminal Justice and Behavior* 16, no. 3 (September 1989): p. 272.

31. James Frank, et al., "Police Attitudes toward DUI Legislation," *Journal of Police Science & Administration* (December 1987): 307.

32. Acker, "Social Sciences," p. 385; John R. Snortum, "Controlling the Alcohol-Impaired Driver in Scandinavia and the United States: Simple Deterrence and Beyond," *Journal of Criminal Justice* 12, no. 2 (1984): 141.

33. Frank P. Williams and E. Lynn White, "Legislative Actions against Drunken Driving: An Assessment with Additional Evidence on the Open Container," *Criminal Justice Policy Review* 1, no. 3 (October 1986): 289; Acker, "Social Sciences," p. 385.

34. Allan R. Meyers et al., "Cops and Drivers: Police Discretion and the

Enforcement of Maine's 1981 OUI law," *Journal of Criminal Justice* 15, no. 5 (1987): 362.

35. Bonnie Steinbock, "Drunk Driving," *Philosophy and Public Affairs* 14, no. 3 (1985): 292.

36. Little, "Drinking, Driving," p. 280.

37. Lanza-Kaduce, "Perceptual," p. 334.

38. John R. Snortum, "Controlling the Alcohol-Impaired Driver in Scandinavia and the United States: Simple Deterrence and Beyond," *Journal of Criminal Justice* 12, no. 2 (1984): 142.

39. Snortum and Berger, "Drinking," p. 486.

40. Snortum, "Controlling," p. 142.

41. Snortum and Berger, "Drinking," p. 486.

42. *Ibid.;* Lanza-Kaduce, "Perceptual," p. 333.

43. Snortum, "Controlling," p. 142.

Selected Bibliography

Acker, James R. (1989) "Social Sciences and the Criminal Law: A Report on America's War Against Drunk Driving." *Criminal Law Bulletin* (July-August): 376-394.

Ball, Richard A., and J. Robert Lilly. (1986) "The Potential Use of Home Incarceration for Drunken Drivers." *Crime and Delinquency* (April): 224-247.

Campane, Jerome O. (1984) "The Constitutionality of Drunk Driver Roadblocks." *FBI Law Enforcement Bulletin* (July): 24-31.

Changes in Alcohol-Involved Fatal Crashes Associated with Tougher State Alcohol Legislation. (1989) Brookeville, Md.: Sigmastat Inc.

Cicchetti, Carmen A., and Louise A. Enos. (1987) *Driving Under the Influence of Liquor.* Boston: Massachusetts Trial Court.

Community Service As an Alternative Sentence for DUI Convictions. (1987) West Lafayette, Ind.: Purdue University.

Compton, Richard P. (1983) *The Use of Safety Checkpoints for DWI Enforcement.* Washington, D.C.: National Highway Traffic Safety Administration.

Cowan, Thomas A., Lee P. Robbins, and Jacqueline R. Meszaros. (1985) "How Judges View Drunk Driving Laws: A Survey." *Judges' Journal* (fall): 4ff.

Craddick, Robert J. (1984) "Blood-Alcohol Tests: Neville and Its Progeny." *Criminal Law Bulletin* (November-December): 493-520.

The Drunk Driver and Jail: Alternatives to Jail. (1986) Washington, D.C.: National Highway Traffic Safety Administration.

Drunk Driving Laws and Enforcement: An Assessment of Effectiveness. (1986) Washington, D.C.: American Bar Association.

Fatal Accident Reporting System. (1988) Washington, D.C.: National Highway Traffic Safety Administration.

Frank, James, et al. (1987) "Police Attitudes Toward DUI Legislation." *Journal of Police Science and Administration* (December): 307-320.

Gomulkiewicz, Robert W. (1985) "Recognizing the Liability of Social Hosts Who Knowingly Allow Intoxicated Guests to Drive: Limits to Socially Acceptable Behavior." *Washington Law Review* 60: 389-406.

Greenfeld, Lawrence A. (1988) *Drunk Driving.* Washington, D.C.: Bureau of Justice Statistics.

Hingson, Ralph, et al. "Legal Interventions to Reduce Drunken Driving and Related Fatalities among Youthful Drivers." *Alcohol, Drugs and Driving* 4: 87-98.

Jailing Drunk Drivers: Impact on the Criminal Justice System, Executive Summary (1985). Washington, D.C.: National Institute of Justice.

Joksch, Hans C. (1988) *The Impact of Severe Penalties on Drinking and Driving.* Washington, D.C.: AAA Foundation for Traffic Safety.

Jones, Jeffrey E. (1986) "The Constitutionality of Sobriety Checkpoints." *Washington and Lee Law Review* (Fall): 1469-1497.

Kilpack, Lloyd (1987) "Use of a Video Camera for DUI Investigations." *FBI Law Enforcement Bulletin* (May): 7-9.

Lanza-Kaduce, Lonn. (1988) "Perceptual Deterrence and Drinking and Driving among College Students." *Criminology* (May): 321-341.

LeClair, Daniel P. (1987) *The Use of Prison Confinement for the Treatment of Multiple Drunken Driver Offenders: An Evaluation of the Longwood Treatment Center.* Boston, Mass.: Massachusetts Department of Correction.

Little, Joseph W. (1980) "Drinking, Driving and the Law." *Criminal Justice Abstracts* (June): 261-288.

McAllister, Ray. (1988) "The Drunken Driving Crackdown: Is It Working?" *American Bar Association Journal* (September): 52-55.

Meyers, Allan R., and Timothy Heeren. (1989) "Discretionary Leniency in Police Enforcement of Laws Against Drinking and Driving." *Journal of Criminal Justice* 17: 179-186.

Meyers, Allan R., et al. (1987) "Cops and Drivers: Police Discretion and the Enforcement of Maine's 1981 OUI law." *Journal of Criminal Justice* 15: 361-368.

Mlsna, Laurie A. (1986) "Public Outcry v. Individual Rights: Right to Counsel and the Drunk Driver's Dilemma." *Marquette Law Review* (Winter): 278-305.

Pierson, Grant, (1987) "Server vs. Driver Liability: A Suggested Change to Reduce Drinking and Driving." *Northern Illinois University Law Review* (Spring): 257-278.

Presidential Commission on Drunk Driving, Final Report. (1982).

Rogers, Lance J. (1985) "The Drunk-Driving Roadblock: Random Seizure or Minimal Intrusion? *Criminal Law Bulletin* (May-June): 197-216.

Ross, H. Laurence. (1987) "Britain's Christmas Crusade Against Drinking and Driving." *Journal of Studies on Alcohol* 48: 476-482.

Ross, H. Laurence, and James P. Foley. (1987) "Judicial Disobediance of the Mandate to Imprison Drunk Drivers." *Law and Society Review* 21: 315-323.

Sauls, John G. (1989) "Traffic Stops: Police Powers under the Fourth Amendment." *FBI Law Enforcement Bulletin* (October): 27-32.

Smith, Carla K. (1983) "Social Host Liability for Injuries Caused by the Acts of an Intoxicated Guest." *North Dakota Law Review* 59: 445-477.

Snortum, John R. (1984) "Controlling the Alcohol-Impaired Driver in Scandinavia and the United States: Simple Deterrence and Beyond." *Journal of Criminal Justice* 12: 131-148.

Sparlin, Derry D. (1986) "Social Host Liability for Guests Who Drink and Drive: A Closer Look at the Benefits and the Burdens." *William and Mary Law Review* (Spring): 583-632.

Standardized Field Sobriety Testing. (1987) Gaithersburg, Md.: International Association of Chiefs of Police.

Surgeon General Workshop on Drunk Driving: Proceedings. (1988) Rockville, Md.: U.S. Department of Health and Human Services.

Sykes, Gary W. (1984) "Saturated Enforcement: The Efficacy of Deterrence and Drunk Driving." *Journal of Criminal Justice* 12: 185-197.

Vingilis, Evelyn R., and Katherine De Genova. (1984) "Youth and the Forbidden Fruit: Experiences with Changes in Legal Drinking Age in North America." *Journal of Criminal Justice* 12: 161-172.

Voas, Robert B. (1986) "Evaluation of Jail as a Penalty for Drunk Driving." *Alcohol, Drugs and Driving* 2: 47-70.

Votey, Harold L. (1984) "The Deterioration of Deterrence Effects of Drunk Driving Legislation." *Journal of Criminal Justice* 12: 115-130.

Williams, Frank P., and E. Lynn White. (1986) "Legislative Actions Against Drunken Driving: An Assessment with Additional Evidence on the Open Container." *Criminal Justice Policy Review* 1: 286-304.

Zeroing In On Repeat DWI Offenders, Conference On Recidivism: A Summary of the Proceedings. (1986) Atlanta, Ga.: National Commission Against Drunk Driving.

Index

About the Author

GERALD D. ROBIN is Professor of Criminal Justice at the University of New Haven. His previous works include *Introduction to the Criminal Justice System* as well as over 30 articles in leading criminology, criminal justice, and sociological journals.